International Company Law

Rino Siffert
Ph.D., attorney-at-law and public notary, LL.M. (Cornell)
Certified Computer Scientist NDL
Lecturer at the Sorbonne-Assas International Law School / Panthéon-Assas Université International (Dubai Campus)

Copyright © 2024 Rino Siffert

All rights reserved.

ISBN: 9798372012769

Foreword

In the world as globalized as it is nowadays, it is almost impossible to imagine an economy without international acting companies and their cross-border transactions as well as their investments. Thus, they have to be considered as an important economic factor.

The content of this book is the result of my professional experience from various capacities in which I dealt with companies doing cross-border transactions and investments. The book is not intended to present an absolutely comprehensive manuscript of all legal aspects in this field; rather, it gives a general review of important issues which a company may encounter in an international context. The purpose was to give a sort of checklist for these issues and to refer to legal sources, which help to find more detailed and profound answers to various problems that derive from companies doing cross-border transactions and investments.

My intent was that the book can be used as a textbook for introductory classes at law faculties, but also as a starting point for legal practitioners and companies.

Fribourg/Switzerland, May 2024

Table of contents

Foreword	III
Table of contents	IV
Abbreviations	XIII
Literature	XV

I.	Introduction			1
II.	Companies in private international law			3
	1.	Generally		3
	2.	Jurisdiction		5
		2.1.	Generally	5
		2.2.	The various jurisdictions of Swiss international company law	7
	3.	Applicable Law		8
		3.1.	Theories of affiliation	8
		3.2.	Solution in the PILA	10
	4.	Recognition of decisions subject to company law		13
		4.1.	Generally	13
		4.2.	Recognition of foreign judgments concerning corporate law claims	15
		4.3.	Recognition of foreign judgments on public issue claims	15
	5.	Branches of foreign companies in another state		16
	6.	Cross-border transfer of the seat of a company / cross-border conversions		18
		6.1.	Generally	18
		6.2.	Transfer of the company from abroad to Switzerland	21
		6.3.	Transfer of the Company from Switzerland to a Foreign Country	23
	7.	Cross-border mergers and demergers		23
		7.1.	Generally	23
		7.2.	Merger	25
		7.3.	Divisions/Demergers	30
III.	Companies in public international law			33
	1.	Generally		33
	2.	Sources of public international law		33
		2.1.	Generally	33
		2.2.	Conventions	34

	2.3.	International custom............................	36
2.4.	General principles..		37
	2.5.	Judicial decisions	38
	2.6	Teachings of the most highly qualified publicists of the various nations	38
3.	Historical background of foreign investment law...		38
4.	State responsibility.......................................		39
	4.1.	Generally...	39
	4.2.	Individuals..	42
	4.3.	Companies...	43
5.	Foreign investment and investment laws........		44
	5.1.	Definition of foreign investment..........	44
		5.1.1. Generally..................................	44
		5.1.2. Foreign direct investments	45
		5.1.3. Foreign portfolio investments ..	45
		5.1.4. Distinction of the kind of investments................................	46
	5.2.	Investments laws.................................	47
		5.2.1. Generally.................................	47
		5.2.2. Domestic investment legislation.................................	47
		5.2.3. Investment treaties	48
	5.3.	Investment contracts between investors and states	51
		5.3.1. Generally..................................	51
		5.3.2. Investor-state contracts.............	52
		5.3.2.1. International-choice-of-law clause	53
		5.3.2.2. Stabilization clause ..	54
		5.3.3. Investors rights under investment conventions............	55
	5.4.	Binding effect of investor-state contracts and investment treaties	55
6.	Remedies in case of violation of public international law		58
	6.1.	Generally...	58
	6.2.	Remedies available to the state	60
		6.2.1. Generally.................................	60
		6.2.2. Restitution in kind....................	61
		6.2.3. Compensation...........................	62

	6.3.	Legal basis for remedies available to the investors	64
		6.3.1. Generally	64
		6.3.2. Remedies provided in an international agreement	64
		6.3.3. Remedies provided in the domestic law of the state responsible for the injury	65
		6.3.4. Remedies provided by investor-state-contracts	65
IV.	Nationalization		66
	1.	Generally	66
	2.	Legality of nationalization	68
		2.1. General rule	68
		2.1.1. Case law	68
		2.1.2. State practice	71
		2.1.3. International instruments	71
		2.2. Public interest/purpose of the nationalization	72
		2.3. Property has been taken following proper law proceedings	74
		2.4. Non-discrimination	75
		2.5. Compensation	75
		2.5.1 Generally	75
		2.5.2. Full compensation v. appropriate compensation	76
		(i) Full compensation	76
		(ii) Appropriate compensation	78
		(iii) Application by tribunals and courts	78
V.	Investment insurance		82
	1.	Generally	82
		1.1. State insurance schemes	83
		1.2. Multilateral international insurance scheme	83
		1.3. Private insurance schemes	83
		1.4. Combination of these types of insurances	84
	2.	MIGA (Multilateral Investment Guarantee Agency)	84
		2.1. Generally	84
		2.2. Purpose	85

		2.3.	Eligible insureds	86
		2.4.	Eligible host countries	86
		2.5.	Insured investments	86
		2.6.	Insurable risks	87
			2.6.1. Generally	87
			2.6.2. Currency inconvertibility and transfer restriction	88
			2.6.3. Expropriation	88
			2.6.4. Breach of contract	89
			2.6.5. War, terrorism and civil disturbance	89
			2.6.6. Non-honoring of financial obligations	90
		2.7.	Duration	91
		2.8.	Premium	91
	3.	Private insurance schemes		91
VI.	Unification of commercial law for international trade and cross border investments			92
	1.	Generally		92
	2.	Organizations/Commissions		92
	3.	Conventions of importance for international trade and cross border business transactions		94
		3.1.	UN Convention on contracts for the international sale of goods (CISG)	94
		3.2.	Convention on the limitation period in the international sale of goods	96
VII.	Legal issues of cross-border joint ventures			99
	1.	Generally		99
	2.	Types of joint ventures		100
		2.1.	Contractual joint venture	100
		2.2.	Equity joint venture	100
	3.	Reasons for a joint venture		100
	4.	Joint venture agreement		102
		4.1.	Generally	102
		4.2.	Definitions	102
		4.3.	Objective of the joint venture	103
		4.4.	Contributions of the parties	103
		4.5.	Organization and management of the joint venture	103
		4.6.	New parties	104
		4.7.	Termination of the joint venture	104

		4.8.	Choice-of-law-clause	104
		4.9.	Dispute resolution mechanism	104
	5.	Tax issues		105
	6.	Competition law issues		105
VIII.	Corporate social responsibility (CSR) and international investments			107
	1.	Generally		107
	2.	Benefits of CSR		108
	3.	International CSR standards		109
		3.1.	Generally	109
		3.2.	OECD Declaration on international investment and multinational enterprises	110
		3.3.	UN Guiding Principles on Business and Human Rights	111
		3.4.	UN Global Compact	112
		3.5.	ISO 26000 Guidance on Social Responsibility	113
		3.6.	Global Reporting Initiative	114
		3.7.	ILO-Standards	114
		3.8.	2030 Agenda for Sustainable Development (UN development goals)	115
		3.9.	EU Strategy for Corporate Social Responsibility	116
		3.10.	G7	116
		3.11.	TCFD	116
		3.12.	Paris Agreement	117
		3.13.	UN Convention on Transnational Corporations and Human Rights	118
		3.14.	Unidroit	119
	4.	Multinational legislation		119
		4.1.	Generally	119
		4.2.	Corporate Sustainability Due Diligence Directive	120
			4.2.1. Generally	120
			4.2.2. Scope of application, risk-based approach and transition plan	120
			4.2.3. Due diligence obligations	121
			4.2.4. Fines and compensation of victims	121

		4.3.	Corporate Sustainability Reporting Directive..	121
			4.3.1. Generally..............................	121
			4.3.2. New terminology	123
			4.3.3. Scope of application	123
			4.3.4. Clarification of the so-called "dual materiality".....	124
			4.3.5. More detailed disclosures on the nature of information	124
			4.3.6. Standards for sustainability reporting..............................	125
			4.3.7. External verification of sustainability reporting	126
			4.3.8. Mandatory reporting in the management report; uniform electronic reporting format..................	126
			4.3.9. Sanctions.............................	126
			4.3.10 Diversity concept................	127
		4.4.	Effects of the EU Corporate Sustainability Due Diligence and Reporting Directives on Companies from Non-EU Member States	127
IX.	International insolvency law....................................			128
	1.	Basics of international insolvency law........		128
	2.	Definitions...		129
		2.1	Insolvency	129
		2.2.	Insolvency proceedings.....................	129
		2.3.	Bankruptcy proceedings....................	130
		2.4.	Moratorium proceedings	131
	3.	International Insolvency Law......................		132
		3.1.	Generally	132
		3.2.	International insolvency procedural law	132
		3.3.	International insolvency conflict of laws	133
	4.	Basic concepts of international insolvency law...		133
		4.1	Territoriality vs. universality............	133
			4.1.1. Principle of territoriality	133
			4.1.2. Principle of universality......	134
			4.1.3. Mediating concepts.............	136
		4.2	Types of insolvency proceedings	137

		4.2.1.	Main insolvency proceedings	137
		4.2.2.	Particular insolvency proceedings	138
5.	Sources of law			140
	5.1	Autonomous Law (Overview)		140
	5.2	Convention/Treaties and European Secondary Legislation		141
		5.2.1.	Istanbul Convention	141
		5.2.2.	EU Insolvency Regulation	142
		5.2.3.	Bilateral Agreements	143
	5.3	Non-binding multinational regulations		143
		5.3.1.	UNCITRAL Model Law on Cross-Border Insolvency	143
		5.3.2.	UNCITRAL Legislative Guide on Insolvency Law	144
6.	Unified International Insolvency Law: EU Insolvency Regulation and UNCITRAL Insolvency Model Law			145
	6.1.	EU Insolvency Regulation		145
		6.1.1.	Background and Objectives	145
		6.1.2.	Scope of application	145
		6.1.3.	Jurisdiction for main and secondary insolvency proceedings	147
		6.1.4.	Effects of recognition and secondary proceedings	152
		6.1.5.	Recognition of judgments related to insolvency	154
		6.1.6.	Applicable Law	155
7.	UNCITRAL Model Law on Cross-border Insolvency			156
	7.1.	Background and subject matter		156
	7.2.	Main Features of the UNCITRAL Model Law		157
		7.2.1.	Generally	157
		7.2.2.	Access of foreign bankruptcy trustees and creditors	158
		7.2.3.	Recognition of foreign insolvency proceedings	160
		7.2.4.	Cross-border cooperation	163

		7.2.5.	Coordination of parallel insolvency proceedings	164

X.	Cross-border company structures				166
	1.	Introduction			166
	2.	Internationalization			167
		2.1.	Generally		167
		2.2.	Company		167
		2.3.	Internationalized Company		167
	3.	Forms of internationalization			168
	4.	Stage theory			170
	5.	Operational organizational structures			172
		5.1.	Generally		172
		5.2.	Non-specific organizational structure		173
		5.3.	Differentiated organizational structure		173
		5.4	Integrated organizational structure		175
			5.4.1.	Generally	175
			5.4.2.	Integrated functional structure	175
			5.4.3.	Integrated product structure	176
			5.4.4.	Integrated regional structure	177
			5.4.5.	Multidimensional structures	177
			5.4.6.	International holding	179
			5.4.7.	Network structure	180
		5.5.	Statutory organizational structures		180
			5.5.1.	Generally	180
			5.5.2.	Foreign branch office	181
			5.5.2.	Foreign subsidiary	182
	6.	Groups of companies			183
		6.1.	Generally		183
		6.2.	Management principle		183
		6.3.	Group structures		184
			6.3.1.	Generally	184
			6.3.2.	Parent company structure	184
			6.3.3.	Holding structure	185
			6.3.4.	Management company	185
			6.3.5.	Divisional groups	185
		6.4.	Types of corporate groups		186
		6.5.	Group of companies considered as one legal entity vs. piercing the corporate veil		187
			6.5.1.	Generally	187

XI

		6.5.2.	Anglo-Saxon Law	187
		6.5.3.	European Law	191
		6.5.4.	Swiss Law	193
7.	Power of multinational companies			194
	7.1.	Generally		194
	7.2.	The veil of incorporation		194
	7.3.	Large-scale production		195
	7.4.	Extraterritoriality		195

Abbreviations

BIT	Bilateral Invetment Treaty
Cf.	Confer
CISG	United Nations Convention on Contracts for the International Sale of Goods
cit.	cited/citation
Coface	Compagnie Française d'Assurance pour le Commerce Extérieur
CSR	Corporate social responsibility
e.g.	Exempli gratia/for example
ECGD	Export Credits Guarantee Department
ECJ	European Court of Justice
ECT	Energy Charter Treaty
EEA	European Economic Area
Et seq.	Et sequens/and the following
EU	European Union
FATF	Financial Action Task Force
FSB	Financial Stability Board
G7	Groupe of Seven
GAFI	Groupe d'action financière
GATT	General Agreement on Tariffs and Trade
GRI	Global Reporting Initiative
i.e.	Id est/that is
IBRID	International Bank for Reconstruction and Development
ICJ	International Court of Justice
ICSID	International Centre for Investment Disputes
IMF	International Monetary Fund
ISO	International Organization for Standardization
MIGA	Multilateral Investment Guarantee Agency

MIT	Multilateral Investment Treaty
NAFTA	North American Free Trade Agreement
NDC	Nationally Determined Contribution
No.	Number
OAS	Organization of American States
OECD	Organisation for Economic Co-operation and Development
op. cit.	Opus citatum/work cited
p./pp.	page/pages
PILA	Swiss Federal Act on Private international Law of December 18, 1987
SMEs	Small and medium sized enterprises
TCFD	Task Force on Climate-related Financial Disclosures
UN	United Nations
UNCITRAL	United Nations Commission on International Trade Law
UNHRC	United Nations Human Rights Council
UNIDROIT	International Institute for the Unification of Private Law
USA	United States of America
USD	United States Dollar
VCLT	Vienna Convention on the Law of Treaties
Vol.	Volume
WTO	World Trade Organization

Literature

AHMED PRISCILLA A./FANG XINGHAI, Project finance in developing countries: IFC's lessons of experience (1999)

AHMED SAHID, Foreign direct investment, trade and economic growth: An introduction, in: Foreign direct investment, trade and economic growth, exploring challenges and opportunities, edited by Sahid Ahmed (2013)

AKEHURST MICHAEL, Custom as a source of international law, British Year Book of International Law (1976)

AKSAMOVIC DUBRAVKA, Transfer of Corporate Seat in EU: Recent Developments, in: Athens Journal of Law, Volume 5, Issue 4 (2019)

ALBANIA BUSINESS AND INVESTMENT OPPORTUNITIES YEARBOOK, Volume 1, Strategic, practical information and opportunities, (2016)

ALVAREZ JOSÉ ENRIQUE, The public international law regime governing international investment (2011)

ASOZU AMAZU A., International commercial arbitration and African States: practice, participation and institutional development (2001)

AUST ANTHONY, Modern treaty law and practice (2000)

BABU R. RAJESH, Remedies under the WTO legal system 2012)

BAETENS FREYA, Investment law within international law: integrationist perspectives (2013)

BAKER J. CRAIG, International law and international relations (2000)

BANKAS ERNEST K., The state immunity controversy in international law, private suits against sovereign states in domestic courts (2005)

BEGIC TAIDA, Applicable law in international investment disputes (2005)

BLAINE HARRISON G., Foreign direct investment (2009)

BÖHLHOFF KLAUS/ BUDDE JULIUS, Company Groups – The EEC proposal for a ninth directive in the light of the legal situation in the Federal Republic of Germany, in:

Journal of Comparative Business and Capital Market Law 6 (1984)

BOPP LUKAS, Sanierung im Internationalen Insolvenzverfahren der Schweiz (2004)

BORN GARY B., International commercial arbitration, volume 1 (2009)

BOULLE LAURENCE, The law of globalization: an introduction (2009)

BREAU SUSAN, Questions & answers, international law 2013 and 2014 (2013)

BUCKLEY PETER J./NEWBOULD GERALD D./ THURWELL JANE, Foreign direct investment by smaller UK firms: the success and failure of first-time investors abroad (1988)

BULJEVICH ESTEBAN C./PARK YOON S., Project financing and the international financial markets (1999)

BULT-SPIERING MIRJAM/DEWULF GEERT, Strategic issues in public-private partnerships, an internal perspective (2006)

BUMB BALU L., Privatization of agribusiness input markets, in: Privatization and deregulation, needed policy reforms for agribusiness development, edited by Surjit S. Sidhu/Mohinder S. Mudahar (1999)

BUTLER STUART, Privatization for public purposes, in: Privatization and its alternatives, edited by William T. Gromley, Jr. (1991)

COLLINS DAVID, An introduction of international investment law (2017) (cit. COLLINS, International investment law)

COLLINS DAVID, The BRIC states and outward foreign direct investment (2013) (cit. COLLINS, BRIC states)

COOK PAUL, Private sector development strategy in developing countries, in: Privatization and market development, global movements in public policy ideas, edited by Graeme Hodge (2006)

COUVREUR PHILIPPE, The international court of justice and the effectiveness of international law (2017)

CUTLER A. CLAIRE, International commercial arbitration, transnational governance, and the new constitutionalism, in: International arbitration & global governance,

Contending theories and evidence, edited by Walter Mattli/Thomas Dietz (2014)

DAHM GEORG/DELBRÜCK JOST/WOLFRUM RÜDIGER, Völkerrecht, volume I/3 (2013)

DAVISON MARK J./MONOTTI ANN L./WISEMAN LEANNE, Australian intellectual property law (2016)

DAWSON FRANK G./WESTON BURNS H., "Prompt, adequate and effective": a universal standard of compensation?, in: 30 Fordham L. Rev. (1962)

DE BRABANDERE ERIC, Investment treaty arbitration as public international law, procedural aspects and implications (2014) (cit. DE BRABANDERE, Investment treaty arbitration)

DE BRABANDERE ERIC, The settlement of investment disputes in the energy sector, in: Foreign investment in the energy sector, Balancing private and public interests, edited by Eric De Brabandere/Tarcisio Gazzini (2014) (cit. DE BRABANDERE, Settlement of investment disputes)

DE LUCA NICOLA, European Company Law, 2nd edition (2021)

DERAINS YVES/SCHWARTZ ERIC A., A guide to the ICC rules of arbitration (2005)

DESSEMONTET FRANÇOIS/ STOFFEL WALTER, Private International Law (Undated)

DESSISLAV DOBREV, Reforming international investments laws: Is it time for a new international social contract to rebalance the investor-state regulatory dichotomy?, in: Yearbook on international investment law & policy 2014 – 2015, edited by Andrea K. Bjorklund (2016)

DIMATTEO LARRY A., International business law and the legal environment: a transactional approach (2017)

DIMSEY MARIEL, The resolution of international investment disputes, Challenges and solutions (2008)

DINAVO JACQUES V., Privatization in developing countries, its impact on economic development and democracy (1995)

DINE JANET/KOUTSIAS MARIOS, Company Law (2020)

DIXON MARTIN, Textbook on international law (2013)

DOLZER RUDOLPH/SCHREUER CHRISTOPH, Principles of international investment law (2012)

DRENCKHAN HEIKE, Grenzüberschreitende Unternehmensstrukturen, in: Handbuch Internationales Handels- und Wirtschaftsrecht, Rechtliche Herausforderungen im Auslandsgeschäft (2015)

DRUEY JEAN NICHOLAS/DRUEY JUST EVA/GLANZMANN LUKAS, Handels- und Gesellschaftsrecht (2010)

DUFFY JOHN W., Andean and Caribbean basin financing directory (1994)

DUGAN CHRISTOPHER F./WALLACE JR. DON/ RUBINS NOAH D./ SABAHI BORZU, Investor-state arbitration (2013) (cit. DUGAN/WALLACE, JR./RUBINS/SABAHI, Investor-state arbitration 2013)

DUGAN CHRISTOPHER F./WALLACE JR. DON/RUBINS NOAH D./ SABAHI BORZU, Investor-State arbitration (2011) (cit. DUGAN/WALLACE JR./RUBINS/SABAHI, Investor-state arbitration 2011)

DUMOI AGUSMAN DAMOS, Treaties under Indonesian law: A comparative study (2014)

EBERLE RETO, Handkommentar Kommentar Schweizerisches Privatrecht (2016)

EGERTON-VERNON JAMES, Is investment treaty arbitration a mechanism to second-guess governments' exercise of administrative discretion: public law or lex investoria?, in: Investment treaty arbitration and international law, edited by Ian A. Laird, Borzu Sabahi/Frédéric G. Sourgens/Todd J. Weiler (2015)

EL-HOSSENY FAROUK, Civil society in investment treaty arbitration, status and prospects (2018)

ENDICOTT MARTIN, The definition of investment in ICSID arbitration: Development lessons for the WTO?, in: Sustainable development in world trade law, edited by Markus W. Gehring/Marie-Claire Cordon (2005)

ENE CHARLOTTE, The Cross-Border Conversion-A Possible Solution for the Mobility of Companies in European Union, Perspectives of Law and Public Administration, 9(1) (2020)

EUROPEAN COMMISSION, SMES OBSERVATORY REPORT 2003/4

FILLERS ALEKSANDERS, Free Movement of Companies After the Polbud Case, European Business Organization Law Review, 21 (2020)

FORD ALAN W., The Anglo-Iranian oil dispute of 1951-1952: a study of the role of law in the relations of states (1954)

FRIEDLAND PAUL D., Arbitration clauses for international contracts (2007)

GASSMANN RICHARD/BOMMER FLORIAN, Handbuch Internationales Handels- und Wirtschaftsrecht, Rechtliche Herausforderungen im Auslandsgeschäft (2015)

GAZZINI TARCISIO, Interpretation of international investment treaties (2016)

GOOZNER MERRILL, The ten largest global business corruption cases, in: The Fiscal Times, December 13, 2011

GRAY CHRISTINE D., Judicial remedies in international law (1990)

GREENIDGE CARL B., Privatization in Ghana, in: Privatization, a global perspective, edited by V. V. Ramanadham (1993)

GUNNAR GROH/RAFFAEL NATH/JULIA KRAFT, Fälle zum Internationalen Gesellschaftsrecht mit Bezügen zum Europäischen Gesellschaftsrecht (2022)

GUTTERMAN ALAN S., A short course in international joint ventures, how to negotiate, establish and manage an international joint venture (2009) (cit. GUTTERMAN, International joint ventures)

GUTTERMAN ALAN S., The law of domestic and international strategic alliances (1995)

HANS GÜNTHER MEISSNER/STEPHAN GERBER, Die Auslandsinvestitionen als Entscheidungsproblem, Betriebswirtschaftliche Forschung und Praxis, 3/1989

HARDING MAEBH, Conflict of laws (2013)

HAREES LUKMAN, The mirage of dignity on the highways of humans 'progress': - the bystanders' perspective (2012)

HECKSCHEN HERIBERT, Internationales Gesellschaftsrecht, Wirtschaftsrecht kompakt (2018)

HEINEMANN ANDREAS/SCHNYDER ANTON K., Internationales Wirtschaftsrecht (2017)

HEPBURN JARROD, Domestic law in international investment arbitration (2017)

HIRSCH MOSHE, Interactions between investment and non-investment obligations, The Oxford handbook of international investment law, edited by Peter Muchlinski/Federico Ortino/Christoph Schreuer (2008)

HIRSCH MOSHE, Sources of international investment law, International investment law and soft law, edited by ANDREA K. Bjorklund/August Reinisch (2012)

HOFFMANN SCOTT L., The law and business of international project finance: a resource for governments, sponsors, lenders, lawyers, and project participants (2001)

HOLLIS DUNCAN B., Sources in interpretation theories, in: The Oxford handbook on the sources of international law, edited by Jean D'Aspremont/Samantha Besson/Séverine Knuchel (2017)

HOLTBRÜGGE DIRK, Internationale Unternehmen, Organisation, in: Georg Schreyögg/Axel von Werder, Enzyklopädie der Betriebswirtschaftslehre/HWO – Handwörterbuch Unternehmensführung und Organisation (2004)

HOLZER MARC/PRICE BYRON E./KANG HWANG-SUN, Public productivity handbook, edited by Marc Holzer/Seok-Hwan Lee (2004)

INKSTER IAN, Intellectual property, information and divergences in economic development – institutional patterns and outcomes circa 1421–2000, in: The role of intellectual property rights in biotechnology innovation, edited by David Castle (2009)

INTERNATIONAL LABOUR ORGANIZATION, sectoral activities programme, terms of employment and working conditions in health sector reforms, JMHSR/1998

INTERNATIONAL MONETARY FUND, Foreign private investment in developing countries (1985)

JACOBS VERNON K./FOX N. RICHARD, Risk management for amateur investors, A guide to higher yields with less risk for nonprofessional investors, plus an analysis of the impact of the new tax law on investors (2003)

JIMÉNEZ DE ARÉCHAGA EDUARDO, Interview: November 1993, in: Five Masters of International Law (2011)

JOHN KENNEDY M. MARIA, International economics (2014)

JOHNSTON R. BARRY/ÖTKER-ROBE İNCI, A modernized approach to managing the risks in cross-border capital movements, IMF Policy Working Paper No. 99/6 (1999)

JOLANTA KREN KOSTIKIEWICZ/RODRIGO RODRIGUEZ, Internationales Insolvenzrecht (2013)

JOYNER CHRISTOPHER C., International law in the 21st century, Rules for global governance (2005)

KÄHR MICHEL, in: Internationales Privatrecht, Grundkurs (2011)

KARSTEN ENGSIG SØRENSEN, Groups of Companies in the Case Law of the Court of Justice of the European Union, in: European Business Law Review Volume 27, Issue 3 (2016)

KINDLER MIKE, in: Internationales Privatrecht, Grundkurs (2011)

KJELDGAARD-PEDERSEN ASTRID, The international legal personality of the individual (2018)

KOJIMA KIYOSHI, Direct foreign investment, A Japanese model of multinational business operations (2010)

KRAYENBUEHL THOMAS E., Cross-border exposures and country risk: Assessment and Monitoring (2001)

KREIKEBAUM HARTMUT/GILBERT DIRK/REINHARDT GLENN O., Organisationsmanagement internationaler Unternehmen, Grundlagen und Strukturen (2002)

KREUZER KARL F., Legal aspects of international joint ventures in agriculture (1990)

KUNZ PETER V., Wirtschaftsrecht – das unbekannte Rechtsgebiet, in: Jusletter December 19, 2022

KUTSCHKER MICHAEL/SCHMID STEFAN, Internationales Management (2011), p. 466 et seq.; RALPH LEHMANN, Internationale Marktschliessung, in: Paul Ammann/Ralph Lehmann/Samuel Van den Berg/Christian Hauser, Going International (2012)

LEITE GUILHERME/ALVES RODRIGUES TALITA, Brazil, in: International joint ventures, the comparative law yearbook of international business, Special issue, edited by Dennis Campbell (2008)

LEPARD BRIAN D., Customary international law, a new theory with practical applications (2010)

LEW JULIAN D. M./MISTELIS LOUKAS A./KRÖLL STEFAN M., Comparative international commercial arbitration (2003)

LIM C. L./HO JEAN/PAPARINSKIS MARTINS, International investment law and arbitration (2018)

LINDBERG VAN, Intellectual property and open source: a practical guide to protecting code (2008)

LO CHANG-FA, Treaty interpretation under the Vienna Convention on the Law of Treaties (2017)

LOWENFELD ANDREAS F., International economic law (2002)

LUO YADONG, Multinational enterprises in emerging markets (2002)

MABABYA MAMARINTA P., The role of multinational companies in the Middle East: the case of Saudi Arabia (2002)

MAGAZINE "*BILANZ*", Zurich 2010

MAKONDO T., Privatisation as a major reform in public sector management, in: Public finance fundamentals, edited by Kabelo Moeti et al. (2007)

MCCORMICK MYLES/SHEPPARD DAVID, Egypt to pay Spanish-Italian JV $2bn in natural gas dispute, in: Financial Times, September 3, 2018

MCILWRATH MICHAEL/SAVAGE JOHN, International arbitration and mediation: A practical guide (2010)

MEINERS ROGER E./RINGLEB AL. H./EDWARDS FRANCES L., The legal environment of business (2018)

MERNA TONY/NJIRU CYRUS, Financing infrastructure projects (2002)

MILLER ROBERT/ GLEN JACK/JASPERSEN FRED/KARMOKOLIAS YANNIS, International joint ventures in developing countries, in: Finance & Development, March 1997

MODY ASHOKA, in: Infrastructure delivery: new ideas, big gains, no panaceas, in: Infrastructure delivery, private initiative and the public good, edited by Ashoka Mody (1996)

NADAKAVUKAREN SCHEFER KRISTA, International investment law, text, cases and materials (2016)

NAKAGAWA JUNJI, Nationalization, natural resources and international investment law, contractual relationship as a dynamic bargaining process (2018)

NDE FRU VALENTINE, The international law on foreign investments and host economies in Sub Saharan Africa, Cameroon, Nigeria, and Kenya (2010)

NEWCOMBE ANDREW/PARADELL LUÍS, Law and practice of investment treaties, standards of treatment (2009)

NG'AMBI SANGWANI PATRICK, Resource nationalism in international investment law (2016)

NIEMEYER RALPH T., Germany after capitalism (2012)

NIEUWENHUYS EVA/BRUS MARCEL, Legal, political and economic aspects, in: Multilateral regulation of investment, edited by Eva Nieuwenhuys/Marcel Brus (2001)

NORDSTROM ROBERT J., Assistant Dean and Associate Professor of Law, The Ohio State University, College of Law, Ohio's Borrowing Statute of Limitations - A Quaking Quagmire in a Dismal Swamp, 16 Ohio St. L.J. 183 (1955)

NWOGUGU E. I., The legal problems of foreign investment in developing countries (1965)

OECD INTERNATIONAL INVESTMENT LAW, a changing landscape, a companion volume to international investment perspectives (2005)

OECD POLICY FRAMEWORK FOR INVESTMENT (2015)

OKEDIJI RUTH, New treaty development and harmonization of intellectual property law, in: Trading in knowledge, development perspectives on TRIPS, trade and sustainability, edited by Christophe Bellmann/Graham Dutfield/Ricardo Meléndez-Ortiz (2003)

ONWUAMAEGBU UCHEORA, International dispute settlement mechanisms – Choosing between institutionally supported and ad hoc; and between institutions, in: Arbitration under international investment agreements, a guide to the key issues, edited by Katia Yannaca-Small (2010)

ORAKHELASHVILI ALEXANDER, Peremptory norms and reparation for internationally wrongfully acts, in: Baltic Yearbook of international law, Volume 3, edited by Ineta Ziemle (2003)

ORTINO FEDERICO/MERSADI TABARI NIMA, International dispute settlement: The settlement of investment disputes concerning natural resources – applicable law and standards of review, in: Research handbook on international law and natural resources, edited by Elisa Morgera/Kati Kulovesi (2016)

OVIDIU IOAN DUMITRU, Transfer of seat within European Union, The latest developments on cross-border conversions, mergers and divisions of companies (2021)

PARLETT KATE, Diplomatic protection and the International Court of Justice, in: The development of international law by the international court of justice, edited by Christian J. Tams/James Sloan (2013)

PERLITZ MANFRED, Internationales Management (2004)

PETERS NIEK, The fundamentals of international commercial arbitration (2017)

PHILIPPIN EDGAR/CHÂTELAIN MATHIEU, Fusioni, scissioni, trasferimenti di patrimonio e di sede transfrontalieri, in: Aspetti patrimoniali e di esecuzione forzata nei rapporti transfrontalieri (2015)

PITEL STEPHEN G. A./RAFFERTY NICHOLAS, Conflict of laws (2010)

POLLACK SAMUEL/WATANABE NAOKO, Choosing a branch or subsidiary for overseas expansion (2021)

PRETORIUS FREDERICK/LEJOT PAUL/MCINNIS/ARTHUR ARNER DOUGLAS/FONG-CHUNG HSU BERRY, Project finance for construction and infrastructure, principles and case studies (2008)

PREVOT FRÉDÉRIC/MESCHI PIERRE-XAVIER, Evolution of an international joint venture: the case of a French – Brazilian joint venture, in: Thunderbird International Business Review, Vol. 48(3) (2006)

RASOULI GHAHROUDI MEHDI/HOSHINO YASUO/TURNBULL STEPHEN JOHN, Foreign direct investment, Ownership advantages, firm specific factors, survival and performance (2018)

REPORT OF THE SWISS FEDERAL DEPARTMENT OF JUSTICE, SWISS FEDERAL OFFICE OF JUSTICE ON THE 'DRAFT SUSTAINABILITY OBLIGATIONS EU' AND APPLICABLE LAW SWITZERLAND, November 25, 2022 (cit. REPORT EU/SWITZERLAND-STAINABILITY OBLIGATIONS)

RIPINSKY SERGEY/WILLIAMS KEVIN, Damages in international investment law (2008)

RUBINS NOAH, The notion of 'investment' in international investment arbitration, in: Arbitrating foreign investment disputes, procedural and substantive legal aspects, volume 19, edited by Norbert Horn (2004)

SABAHI BORZU, Compensation and restitution in investor-state arbitration, Principles and practice (2011)

SABAHI BORZU/BIRCH NICHOLAS J., Comparative compensation for expropriation, in: International investment law and comparative public law, edited by Stephan W. Schill (2010)

SALACUSE JESWALD W., The law of investment treaties (2009)

SALACUSE JESWALD W., The three laws of international investment: National, contractual, and international frameworks for foreign capital (2013) (cit. SALACUSE, The three laws of investment treaties)

SATTOROVA MAVLUDA, Reassertion of control and contracting parties' domestic law responses to investment treaty arbitration, between reform, reticence and resistance, in: Reassertion of control over the investment treaty regime, edited by Andreas Kulick (2017)

SCHAFFER RICHARD/AGUSTI FILIBERTO/DHOOGE LUCIEN J., International business law and its environment (2018)

SCHILL STEPHAN W., The backlash against investment arbitration, edited by Michael Waibel/Asha Kaushal/Kyo-Hwa Liz Chung/Claire Balchin (2010)

SCHMALENBACH KIRSTEN, Art. 26 Pacta sunt servanda, in: Vienna Convention on the Law of Treatises, A commentary, edited by Oliver Dörr/Kirsten Schmalenbach (2012)

SCHNYDER ANTON K., Insolvenzrecht Deutschlands und der Schweiz – unter Einbezug der EG-Verordnung Nr. 1346/2000, in: Gottwald Peter, Aktuelle Entwicklungen des europäischen und internationalen Zivilverfahrensrechts: ein Forschungsbericht (2002)

SCHÖBENER BURKHARD/HERBST JOCHEN/PERKAMS MARKUS, Internationales Wirtschaftsrecht (2010)

SCHWEIZTER HEIKE WOESTE KAI, Die Haftung von Konzerngesellschaften im europäischen Wettbewerbsrecht, Der wettbewerbsrechtliche Unternehmensbegriff und seine Legitimationsgrundlagen, in: Vom Konzern zum Einheitsunternehmen (2020)

SHAW MALCOLM N., International law (2017)

SIFFERT RINO, Berner Kommentar Handelsregister (2021)

SIFFERT RINO/PETROVIC SINISA, Legal Aspects of foreign investments in developing countries (2019)

SMITH WARRICK, Covering political and regulatory risks: Issues and options for private infrastructure arrangements, in: Dealing with public risk in private infrastructure, edited by Timothy Irwin/Michael Klein/Guillermo E. Perry/Mateen Thobani (1997)

SOEGAARD GITTE, Cross-border Transfer and Change of Lex Societatis After Polbud, C-106/16: Old Companies Do Not Die... They Simply Fade Away to Another Country, European Company Law, 15(1) (2018)

SORNARAJAH MUTHUCUMARASWAMY, Resistance and change in the international law on foreign investment (2015) (cit. SORNARAJAH, International law)

SORNARAJAH MUTHUCUMARASWAMY, The international law on foreign investment (2010) (cit. SORNARAJAH, Resistance)

STEWART DAVID P., Private international law, the rule of law and economic development, 56. Vill. L. Rev. 607 (2011)

TANG YI SHIN, The international trade policy for technology transfers: legal and economic dilemmas on multilateralism versus bilateralism (2009)

THIRLWAY HUGH, International law and its sources (2014)

THOMPSON ROBERT B., Piercing the Corporate Veil: An Empirical Study, 76 Cornell L. Rev. 1036 (1991)

TILMANN MICHAEL DRALLE, Ownership unbundling and related measures in the EU energy sector, Foundations, the impact of WTO law and investment protection (2018)

TOMUSCHAT CHRISTIAN, Individual reparation claims in instances of grave human rights violations: the position under general international law, in: State responsibility and the individual, edited by Albrecht Randelzhofer/Christian Tomuschat (1999)

TRAKMAN LEON E., Australia's rejection of investor-state arbitration: A sign of global change, in: Regionalism in international investment law, edited by Leon E. Trakman/Nicola W. Ranieri (2013)

TRAKMAN LEON E./RANIERI NICOLAS W., Foreign direct investment: a historical perspective, in: Regionalism inter international investment law, edited by Leon E. Trakman/Nicolas W. Ranieri (2013)

TRISTAN JONES, EU competition law: the liability of group companies for each other's wrongdoing, in: Butterworths Journal of International Banking and Financial Law, March 2019

TRUNK ALEXANDER, Internationales Insolvenzrecht, Systematische Darstellung des deutschen Rechts mit rechtsvergleichenden Bezügen (1998)

UNCITRAL Legislative Guide on Insolvency (2005)

UNDP TANZANIA SUCCESS STORIES, FIGHTING CORRUPTION (2013)

UNITED NATIONS CONFERENCE ON TRADE AND DEVELOPMENT, Word investment report 2007, Transnational corporations, extractive industries and development (2007)

USMAN ADAMU KYUKA, Theory and practice of international economic law (2017)

VAN DE WALLE NICOLAS, Privatization in developing countries: a review of the issues, in: World Development, Vol. 17, No. 5 (1989)

VICARI ANDREA, European Company Law (2021)

VON BÜREN ROLAND, Der Konzern, Rechtliche Aspekte eines wirtschaftlichen Phänomens, Schweizerisches Privatrecht, VIII/6 (2005)

VOON TANIA, The world trade organization, the TRIPS agreement and traditional knowledge: in: Indigenous intellectual property, a handbook of contemporary research, edited by Matthew (2015)

WANG GUIGUO, International investment law: a Chinese perspective (2015)

WARREN HEAD JOHN/FRISCH DAVID, Global business law: principles and practice of international commerce and investment (2007)

WILLMAN JOHN, Nationalisation: a blast from the past, in: Financial Times, January 18, 2018

WONG JARROD, Umbrella clauses in bilateral investment treaties: Of breaches of contract, treaty violations, and the divide between developing and developed countries in foreign investment disputes, 14 Geo. Mason L. Rev. 137 (2006)

WORLD DEVELOPMENT REPORT 1994, Infrastructure for development (1994)

YAN AIMIN / LUO YADONG, International joint ventures, theory and practice (2001)

YEN TRINH HAI, The interpretation of investment treaties (2014)

YOO JOHN/STRADNER IVANA, Customary law today, edited by Laurent Mayali/Pierre Mousseron (2018)

International Company Law

I. Introduction

International company law is an autonomous field of law, notably it is a cross-section of private law as well as public law and is characterized by its focus on the economy.[1] In an interdependent, globalized economy, investments and various transactions of goods, services or resources by companies as an instrument of entrepreneurship are often done across national borders.

In this context, *international company law can be looked at as the various laws, regulations and legal practices that govern numerous issues related to a company in cross-border situations and cross-border business transactions with legal entities, private individuals or even a state.*

Thus, international company law may involve advising companies or multinational corporate groups on legal aspects with regard to countries to which they export goods, in which they provide services, in which they make either

---

[1] PETER V. KUNZ, Wirtschaftsrecht – das unbekannte Rechtsgebiet, in: Jusletter December 19, 2022, pp. 1 et seq.

foreign investments or they enter into joint ventures. By acting on a multinational level companies can be subject to issues related to private and public international law, international insolvency proceedings and corporate social responsibility. Cross-border mobility of companies exposes them to the risk of nationalization or the need to secure their investments or interests with an insurance. Furthermore, cross-border transactions show the importance of unification of commercial law for the international trade by companies.[2]

---

[2] As this book focuses on the teachings given by the author at the "*Sorbonne-Assas International Law School/Panthéon-Assas Université International*", there are no chapters on issues of intellectual property law, tax law and criminal law. These learning contents are completely or at least partly taught in other courses of the program. However, if there is an interest by the reader to know more about intellectual property law and the danger of corruption in relation to international investments by companies, it can be referred to the following book: RINO SIFFERT/SINISA PETROVIC, Legal Aspects of foreign investments in developing countries (2019), pp. 104 et seq. and pp. 144 et seq.

II. Companies in private international law

1. Generally

Case handling in the field of international company law requires first and foremost an understanding of the interplay between the *international private law rules* (*"conflict-of-laws"* or *"collision law"*) and the relevant *substantive law rules*.[3] Each state has its own legal system and thus its own private law (also called *"civil law"*). These differ greatly from one another in terms of content. The legal system of a state regulates almost exclusively domestic matters. The question therefore arises as to how cross-border issues, i.e., issues that have relations to more than one legal system, are to be judged by the court. In order to answer this question, *private international law* can play a major role as it is the legal framework composed of conventions, protocols, laws, legal guides, uniform documents, case law, practice and customs that determines the applicable law regarding a cross-border investment or business transaction of a company.[4] The term *"applicable law"* is a specific notion of private international law and refers to the national law that governs a given question in an international context, i.e., the substantive law. If a dispute arises *over issues related to a company in cross-border situations and business transactions* and there is not a choice-of-court- and/or choice-of-law[5]-clause in a contract, then the competent court will determine based on its own private international law which of two or more conflicting domestic laws should govern the dispute.[6]

---

[3] GUNNAR GROH/RAFFAEL NATH/JULIA KRAFT, Fälle zum Internationalen Gesellschaftsrecht mit Bezügen zum Europäischen Gesellschaftsrecht (2022), p. 3.

[4] DAVID P. STEWART, Private international law, the rule of law and economic development, 56. Vill. L. Rev. 607 (2011), pp. 607 et seq.

[5] Such clauses can be included in a contract between the parties or such an agreement can be made when the dispute between the parties arises. They have to be in writing. If that is the case then the chosen court is exclusively competent and/or the chosen law has to be applied by the court. However, it is possible that the choice of court and the choice of law are mandatorily excluded or limited due to protection considerations. National laws and international agreements state these considerations.

Private international law is known not to be easily understood.

> *"The realm of conflict of laws is a dismal swamp, filled with quaking quagmires, and inhabited by learned but eccentric professors who theorize about mysterious matters in a strange and incomprehensible jargon. The ordinary court, or lawyer, is quite lost when engulfed in it."*[7]

Therefore, this basic system will be briefly presented here in more detail.

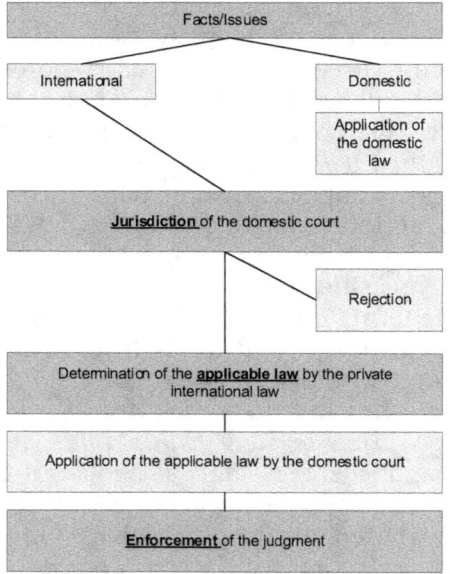

In a dispute involving relations with more than one national legal system, the first question that arises is which court is competent to deal with a case, i.e., does the court have *jurisdiction* to judge the cross-border issue. This question is significant because in the field of international company law

---

[6] Cf. STEPHEN G. A. PITEL/NICHOLAS RAFFERTY, Conflict of laws (2010), p. 212 and 272; MAEBH HARDING, Conflict of laws (2013), pp. 141-142.

[7] Quote by ROBERT J. NORDSTROM, Assistant Dean and Associate Professor of Law, The Ohio State University, College of Law, Ohio's Borrowing Statute of Limitations - A Quaking Quagmire in a Dismal Swamp, 16 Ohio St. L.J. 183 (1955), p. 183.

there is a manifest absence of international treaties or conventions and therefore courts apply very often the rules of private international law of their respective state and determine based on it the applicable law for each case, and, accordingly it may also result in different legal consequences.[8] This shows that the question of the *applicable law* can only be answered once the international jurisdiction of the court has been clarified. Thus, the following notions on private international company law have to be explained based on a national law. Due its simplistic structure and wording the Swiss Federal Act on Private international Law of December 18, 1987 (PILA) will be used for this. The PILA regulates for each subject area (e.g., liability, trusts or company law) the jurisdiction of the Swiss courts and only then determines which law the Swiss court has to apply in the matter itself (e.g., Swiss law or German law). In principle, the application of the PILA does not depend on reciprocity by foreign countries.[9] A judgment can then be enforced in Switzerland by applying the national civil procedure law; abroad, one must first have the judgment recognized and declared enforceable based on international treaties or conventions or the respective national law. The PILA also has specific rules for the *recognition and declaration of enforceability of foreign judgments*.

2. Jurisdiction

2.1. Generally

The international jurisdiction of domestic courts and authorities is regulated – if there is no specific convention or treaty – in the domestic law. For instance, in the EU there is no harmonized *"collision company law"*; and for example, Germany does not have a specific written law. However, there is customary law on these issues.[10] In Switzerland,

---

[8] The term *"international"* does therefore not refer to the source of law, but to the facts of the case.
[9] ANDREAS HEINEMANN/ANTON K. SCHNYDER, Internationales Wirtschaftsrecht in a nutshell (2016), p. 106.
[10] GUNNAR GROH/RAFFAEL NATH/JULIA KRAFT, op. cit., pp. 4 et seq.

each section of the special part of the PILA begins with provisions on the jurisdiction.[11] In order to avoid qualification problems by the court that has to examine a case based on their applicable private international law, the latter often defines the term *"company"* and which kind of legal entities fall under this term. Only if there is not a choice-of-court agreement or clause in the relevant contract and the court reaches the conclusion that the fact pattern and the issue at hand can be looked at as an international *"company matter"*, then the court will apply the relevant legal provisions for determining its jurisdiction. For example, the articles on international company law in the PILA (articles 151 et seq.) will only be applied to an international case if the issues at hand involve *"companies"* in the sense of Art. 150 (1) PILA which are all *"organized associations of persons and organized unit of assets"*.[12] The term *"associations of persons"* refers to such associations that have a common purpose and are based either on a contractual basis or on a registration in a business registry. The term *"unit of assets"* also covers purpose-oriented, independent asset pools which do not have a direct basic personal connection, such as foundations. The definition element *"organized"* does not refer to a legally standardized form, but is to be understood in the sense that a somehow institutionalized form of the association of persons or the unit of assets, which has an external effect, is given. Article 150 (2) PILA[13] contains a provision on the conflict-of-law classification of the legal form of the *"simple partnership"*. Simple partnerships are generally company-like associations of persons. Their wide scope of application due to the various forms and the catch-all function in the substantive law is limited in terms of conflict-of-laws in such a way that the simple partnership is assigned either to

---

[11] FRANÇOIS DESSEMONTET/WALTER STOFFEL, Private International Law (Undated), p. 6.
[12] Article 150 (1) PILA states the following: *"For the purposes of this Act, a company is any organized association of persons and any organized unit of assets."*
[13] Articles 150 (2) PILA states the following: *"Simple partnerships that have not provided themselves with an organization are governed by the provisions of this Act relating to the law applicable to contracts (Art. 116 et seq.)."*

corporate-conflict-of-laws or to contract-conflict-of-laws according to its specific form in the case at hand.

2.2. The various jurisdictions of Swiss international company law

Pursuant to article 151 (1) PILA, in disputes concerning company law, the Swiss courts at the seat of the company have jurisdiction to receive actions against the company, its shareholders or members, or persons liable under company law.

However, next to this general rule there are also the following rules of jurisdiction:
- *Liability of a shareholder/member or a person (article 151 (2) PILA)*:
  In addition to the jurisdiction at the Swiss registered office, article 151 (2) PILA provides for jurisdiction either at the Swiss domicile of the defendant or, in the absence of such domicile, at the habitual residence of the defendant in Switzerland or at the place where the company is administered in fact for actions against a shareholder/member or against a person liable on the basis of liability under company law or against the foreign company for which such person is acting.
- *Place of public issue of equity or debt securities (article 151 (3) PILA)*:
  Disputes regarding liability arising out of the public issue of equity or debt securities may also be brought before the Swiss courts at the place of issue. Due to this special jurisdiction with regard to liability claims, an extension of the jurisdiction according to article 151 (1) and (2) PILA is achieved in favor of the interests of the injured parties for an efficient legal protection. This is a mandatory jurisdiction provision insofar as it cannot be excluded by a choice-of-court agreement.
- *Jurisdiction based on article 159 PILA and article 152 PILA*:
  The special reference in article 159 PILA, which assigns the personal liability of persons acting on behalf of foreign companies under certain conditions to Swiss law for assessment, requires for a meaningful enforcement

the norm-specific jurisdiction contained in article 152 PILA.
- *Protective measures (article 153 PILA)*:
For measures intended to protect assets in Switzerland of a company with its seat abroad, the Swiss judicial or administrative authorities at the place where the assets are located have jurisdiction.

3. Applicable Law

3.1. Theories of affiliation

As we have seen, each legal system has its own private international law that determines for companies the applicable law in an international matter, i.e., the so-called "*company statute*" or "*lex societatis*". Generally speaking, the "*company statute*" is the law that presents the closest relationship or connection with the company in a specific case. Normally, this relationship or connection is defined by detailed and numerous conflicts-of-law rules either in international conventions/treatises or in the national law of a state.[14] Legal issues related to companies are connected or linked by the private international law in different ways (so-called "*connecting factors*").[15] This is strongly related to the fact that it is difficult to manifest the actual center of life of companies. A company can be founded and administered at any place and, within the scope of its activities, be active worldwide. Nevertheless, in the private international law there are two main theories regarding the "*company statute*" that determine the applicable law in legal matters:[16]

- "*Incorporation theory*" (also called "*incorporation doctrine*"):
According to the incorporation theory the law applicable to the company is the law according to which it was founded and, if applicable, registered in a business registry. As a rule, the company usually has its statutory

---

[14] DESSEMONTET/STOFFEL, op. cit., p. 7.
[15] GROH/NATH/KRAFT, op. cit., p. 4.
[16] Cf. also HERIBERT HECKSCHEN, Internationales Gesellschaftsrecht, Wirtschaftsrecht kompakt (2018), p. 8 and GROH/NATH/KRAFT, op. cit., p. 5.

seat in the corresponding state. For the *"incorporation theory"* it is irrelevant where the company is actually administered or where its economic center is located.[17] The link to the statutory-formal seat of the company has the advantage that this is usually fixed regardless of the economic appearance of the company. The *"incorporation theory"* is followed by many foreign legal systems, in particular by the Anglo-American legal system, and also corresponds to the Dutch and Swiss legal conception.[18] The *"incorporation theory"* is also used by Sweden, Finland Malta and most of the East European states like Romania, Bulgaria and Croatia.[19]

- *"Seat theory"* (also called *"real seat theory"* or *"theory of the effective administrative seat"*):
On the other hand, the *"seat theory"* is based on the place of actual administration. In other words, the company is to be governed by the law of the state in which it carries out its main activity.[20] For example, the *"seat theory"* is favorized in Germany, Austria, Belgium, Luxembourg, Greece, Portugal and the Northern East European countries like Latvia, Lithuania and Estonia; however, decisions by the European Court of Justice (ECJ) limit the effects of the *"seat theory"* as based on the freedom of establishment granted in the EU the *"seat theory"* cannot be applied to companies founded in the EU.[21] The application of the *"seat theory"*, however, results in an increasing number of void or legally non-existent companies, since it is regularly required that the company must comply with all mandatory provisions of the country in which it has its seat. This includes also the

---

[17] Cf. MIKE KINDLER, in: Internationales Privatrecht, Grundkurs, (2011), p. 149 and HEINEMANN/SCHNYDER, Internationales Wirtschaftsrecht (2017), p. 101.
[18] HEINEMANN/SCHNYDER, op. cit., p. 101.
[19] OVIDIU IOAN DUMITRU, Transfer of seat within European Union, The latest developments on cross-border conversions, mergers and divisions of companies (2021), pp. 917 et seq.
[20] HECKSCHEN, op. cit., p. 8 and HEINEMANN/SCHNYDER, op. cit., p. 101. Please note that so-called *"mediating theories"* will not be explained here, as they do not really have an independent meaning according to the present view.
[21] DUMITRU, op. cit., pp. 917 et seq. and HECKSCHEN, op. cit., p. 8.

formation requirements. Thus, it becomes clear that the *"seat theory"* in itself only represents a variant of the *"incorporation theory"*, which, however, combines the connecting factors of both theories. The danger that a company is ultimately not legally existing is increased in this way.[22]

> **Racetrack-Decision of the German Federal Supreme Court of October 27, 2008**
> **Case No.: II ZR 158/06**
> A Swiss joint stock corporation administered in Germany was not recognized as such because it had not observed and complied with the formation requirements of the German law. Although the Swiss company was not without rights according to the case law of the German Federal Supreme Court, it could only assert its rights as a (legally capable) partnership under German law. The non-recognition as a joint stock corporation leads to the partners being personally and jointly liable for the company's debts.

3.2. Solution in the PILA

For example, in article 154 (1) PILA the Swiss legislator has opted in principle for the *"incorporation theory"*.[23] Thus, companies are mainly subject to the law of the state according to whose regulations they are created and organized. This fundamental decision for the *"incorporation theory"* serves the purpose of legal certainty, as it is most suitable for guaranteeing the existence of the legal personality of a company. This is also conducive for creditor protection, since creditors can rely on the existence of the company once it has been created. The law of the state of incorporation only applies, however, if the company complies with the publicity and registration requirements of the said state, or - in the absence of such regulations - has organized itself in accordance with the law of that state. If these requirements are not met, the *"seat theory"* is applied

---

[22] Cf. MESSAGE OF THE SWISS FEDERAL COUNCIL 1982, p. 263 and pp. 441 et seq. as well as MIKE KINDLER, op. cit., p. 149.
[23] HEINEMANN/SCHNYDER, op. cit, p. 101.

as a subsidiary rule pursuant to article 154 (2) PILA. In this case, the company is subject to the law of the state in which its actual administration is located.

According to the intention of the Swiss legislator, the company statute should have the broadest possible scope of application. A wide scope of application is necessary due to overriding interests of third parties, in particular for reasons of creditor protection. As an example, article 155 letter a)-i) PILA lists the most important points regulated by the statute. First of all, this includes the legal nature of the company (a). In this respect, the applicable law must determine what type of company has been created and whether the association of persons or the property unit has legal personality. According to the company statute, the question of the formation and the demise is then to be decided (b). This also includes the corresponding procedural regulations (e.g., business registration, liquidation, etc.). In addition to the company name (d) and the organization of the company (e), the relationships between the company and its members (f) as well as liability (g and h) and representation (i) are subject to the applicable law. According to its wording, the list in article 155 PILA is not exhaustive.

As mentioned above, the Swiss legislator intended a broad scope of application of the company statute and drafted accordingly the abovementioned article 155 PILA. In certain areas, however, special rules are appropriate where they serve the overriding interest of third parties. These are standardized in articles 156 et seq. PILA and some will be explained in the following:

– *Equity securities and bonds*:
  Claims arising from the public issue of equity securities and bonds on the basis of prospectuses, circulars or similar announcements are also primarily governed by the company statute. Alternatively, according to article 156 PILA, the law of the state where these instruments were issued may be invoked (*lex loci emissionis*). This alternative connection in the PILA serves to protect those persons who subscribe to securities and bonds on the basis of public offers. As a result, according to article 156 PILA the foreign investor can invoke the foreign law at the place of issuance against the Swiss company.

- *Protection of business name*:
While the creation of a business name follows the company statute, the protection of the business name is separately linked, i.e., there is another connecting factor, in the PILA. Article 157 PILA distinguishes between companies that are registered in one of the Swiss business registries and those that are not. According to article 157 (1) PILA, Swiss law is applied with regard to the protection of business names if the company is registered in one of the various Swiss business registries. Subjecting the protection of business names to domestic law for companies that are registered in one of the Swiss business registries serves legal certainty. All infringements of business names are subject to the law of the place of infringement, i.e., the law of the place of registration. In addition, the legislator based the applicability of Swiss law on the jurisdiction of the tort statute and the territoriality in questions of intellectual property law, as the Federal Supreme Court already did before the PILA came into force. If a company is not registered in Switzerland, the protection of its business name is governed by the law applicable to unfair competition or the law applicable to the infringement of personality rights.
- *Liability for foreign companies*:
Article 159 PILA contains a special connection for the liability for debts of foreign companies and relativizes the *"principle of incorporation"* to a large extent. The main reason for this relativization is the protection of creditors. Imagine, for example, that foreign law does not know any capital protection provisions or does not give the shareholder or the creditor any possibilities to intervene in the relevant cases. Such negative effects of the *"incorporation theory"* are to be prevented by article 159 PILA, according to which the liability of the board of directors/managers of a company incorporated under foreign law is subject to Swiss law if the business of the company is conducted in Switzerland or from Switzerland. The Swiss legislator, who himself describes this provision as an *"unusual norm"*, was thus primarily aiming at so-called *"pro-forma-companies"* incorporated abroad, which only serve the purpose of depriving the creditor of the liability substrate. At first glance, article

159 PILA seems to have arisen from a necessity. It seems logical that creditors must be protected. One could argue that the legislative decision for the primary linkage according to the *"incorporation theory"* would have made such a *"parachute"* necessary. However, a closer look reveals that article 159 PILA causes more injustice and ambiguity than it prevents. To begin with, the provision targets only domestic creditors because of its one-sided wording. Why discrimination against foreign creditors should be justified is not evident. This could certainly not be legitimized by the fear that, with an all-round formulation, foreign law might be applied to Swiss companies if their actual administration is located abroad. Homeland security/protection cannot and must not be the task of the private international law when a foreign trade-related matter as international company law is at issue. According to the view presented here, an extensive interpretation of article 159 PILA is justified for these reasons, especially since its wording does not expressly exclude an appeal by foreign creditors. The possibility of an invocation of article 159 PILA by the foreign creditor will always have to be given if he has trusted in good faith that his contracting party is a Swiss company.

4. Recognition of decisions subject to company law

4.1. Generally

Judgments and other decisions of authorities cannot be recognized and enforced in other states, i.e., outside the state of judgment, without further ado. In this respect, they are not automatically treated the same way as domestic judgments.[24] However in international matters, the prevailing party in a case often has an interest in the judgment being valid and having legal consequences not only in the state of judgment but also in another state. A foreign judgment is an act of sovereignty which, due to the principle of territoriality, is generally limited in its effect to the territory of the state in which the judgment was rendered and therefore has no effect

---

[24] Cf. HEINEMANN/SCHNYDER, op. cit., p. 122.

abroad. Since such a legal situation is unthinkable in today's internationally networked society, and since automatic equal treatment of domestic and foreign judgments is not yet a viable option in view of their possible divergences, it is necessary to regulate which judgments have domestic effects and how. This is done based on a procedure which aims for the recognition[25] or enforcement[26] of the foreign decision. Each state decides for itself whether and under what conditions a foreign decision has domestic effect. In practice, a decision confirming the validity of the judgment within the state must be obtained from the courts of that state.[27]

Regarding the recognition and enforcement of foreign court decisions the primacy of international conventions or treaties must also be taken into account. For example, Switzerland has concluded a large number of international treaties on recognition and enforcement of foreign judgements, in which Switzerland has accepted, in accordance with the principle of reciprocity, to recognize and enforce judgments in accordance with the conditions laid down in the international conventions or treatises. For instance, the Convention on jurisdiction and the recognition and enforcement of judgments in civil and commercial matters was concluded in Lugano initially on October 30, 2007 (also called *"Lugano Convention"*)[28] and it is in Europe of

---

[25] Recognition has the effect of extending the effects of a judgment given in a foreign country (country of judgment) to the domestic country (country of recognition).

[26] Enforcement in the present case concerns the admission of the foreign judgment to domestic enforcement; the domestic means of enforcement are made available to enforce the foreign judgment.

[27] MICHEL KÄHR, Grundriss des Internationalen Zivilprozessrechts, in: Grundriss Internationales Privatrecht (2011), p. 200.

[28] The signatories are the Swiss Confederation, the European Community, the Kingdom of Denmark, the Kingdom of Norway and the Republic of Iceland. It is the successor to the Lugano Convention on jurisdiction and enforcement of judgments in civil and commercial matters of September 16, 1988, which is why it is often referred to as the revised Lugano Convention. At the same time, it also serves as a parallel agreement to Council Regulation (EC) 44/2001 of December 22, 2000 on jurisdiction and the recognition and enforcement of judgments in civil and commercial matters (the Brussels I Regulation), which in turn was replaced by

paramount importance in this respect. Further multilateral treaties have been concluded in the fields of matrimonial law. In addition, there are various bilateral conventions. If no international treaty is applicable, Switzerland has established unilateral rules in the PILA.[29]

The PILA defines the jurisdiction of foreign courts and authorities in every section of its special part. The general provisions state the principle according to which a foreign judgement must be recognized in Switzerland if the defendant has his habitual residence in the state in which the decision was rendered, or if he has submitted to the jurisdiction of this state by a prorogation agreement or tacitly (article 26 PILA). As a rule, recognition does not depend upon reciprocity, except for the recognition of foreign bankruptcy decrees. Recognition may be refused if a party establishes that it was not duly notified of the proceedings or that the decision was rendered in violation of fundamental principles of Swiss procedural law, especially in violation of due process of law, or if, in a general way, recognition would be manifestly incompatible with Swiss public policy (article 27 PILA).[30]

4.2. Recognition of foreign judgments concerning corporate law claims

According to article 165 (1) PILA foreign decisions relating to claims concerning company law are recognized in Switzerland if they were rendered or are recognized in the state of the seat of the company, provided the defendant was not domiciled in Switzerland (a); or if they were rendered in the state of the defendant's domicile or habitual residence (b).

Regulation (EU) 1212/2012 of January 10, 2015. While the Lugano Convention 2007 entered into force for the European Union, Denmark and Norway on January 1, 2010, it has been only applied in Switzerland since January 1, 2011. For Iceland, it entered into force on May 1, 2011. For states that join the European Union after the conclusion of the Lugano Convention, the Convention applies automatically from their EU accession date.

[29] KÄHR, op. cit., p. 202.
[30] DESSEMONTET/STOFFEL, op. cit., p. 8.

4.3. Recognition of foreign judgments on public issue claims

If liability arising from prospectuses, circulars or similar publications regarding public issues of equity or debt securities is the basis of a claim upheld in a foreign judgment, the judgment will be recognized in Switzerland if it was rendered in the state in which the place of issue of the equity or debt securities is located and the defendant was not domiciled in Switzerland (article 165 (2) PILA).

5. Branches of foreign companies in another state

A branch is a direct extension of the main establishment, i.e., the company, that operates usually ongoing business activities on behalf of the main establishment. In many jurisdictions, from a company law perspective, a branch is considered to be part of the company, i.e., the main establishment, and thus, does not have a separate legal personality, i.e., not an own legal personality. For example, in Switzerland, Austria, USA etc., a branch may not enter into an agreement on its own. The main establishment, i.e., the company, will be the contracting party in its capacity as the *"owner"* of the branch. However, in Brazil, that is not the case. Brazilian company law recognizes a separate legal personality of branches, allowing branches to enter into contracts with third parties without having to involve the main establishment. For tax purposes, branches are usually considered as permanent establishments and are therefore subject to taxation in the host state.[31] In many states, foreign companies can establish a branch as long as they are registered in a business registry or a comparable registry in their home state and they register the branch in the competent business registry or a comparable registry of the host state. Of course, the necessary information must be submitted to the registry and the registration fee paid. In some states, the establishment of a branch enables the company to operate in the host state with a more

---

[31] SAMUEL POLLACK/NAOKO WATANABE, Choosing a branch or subsidiary for overseas expansion (2021), p. 2.

streamlined, cost-effective structure than with a subsidiary; however, in some states it is preferable to create a local legal entity in the form of a subsidiary as it is easier to negotiate contracts or to obtain bank accounts. As we have seen above, the establishment of a branch enables foreign companies to create a unit in the host state in order to participate and to act in the host state's market. Very often, such branches have also to obtain a license to trade.

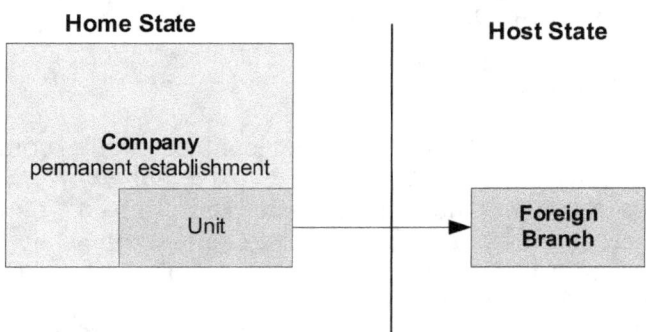

In Switzerland for example, article 160 of the PILA provides for a special connection for branches of foreign companies in Switzerland.[32] According to para. 1, a company with its registered office abroad is in principle entitled to establish a branch in Switzerland. The branch is subject to Swiss law. Thus, there is a uniform regulation in this context.[33] The subordination to domestic law results in an obligation to register the branch in one of the Swiss business registries.[34] The power of representation of the branch of a foreign company is governed by Swiss law (article 160 (2) sentence 1 PILA). The relevant provisions of the foreign company statute are therefore irrelevant with regard to the branch in Switzerland. In addition, at least one person authorized to represent the branch and with it also the company must be resident in Switzerland and registered in the business registry (article 160 (2) sentence 2 PILA). In this regard, the Swiss law is more restrictive than the countries of the EU as for example in Austria the

---

[32] KINDLER, op. cit., p. 153.
[33] MESSAGE OF THE SWISS FEDERAL COUNCIL 1982, p. 263 and p. 445.
[34] Regarding the details for the registration of a Swiss branch it can be referred to article 113 of the Swiss Federal Ordinance on Business Registration (SR 221.411).

requirement to appoint a permanent representative with habitual residence in Austria does not apply to the branch in Austria in the case of foreign companies with their registered office, head office or principal place of business in an EU/EEA state.

6. Cross-border transfer of the seat of a company / cross-border conversions

6.1. Generally

The cross-border transfer of the legal seat of a company (also known as *"re-domiciliation of a company"*) is the process through which a company can shift its domicile from one jurisdiction to another, by changing the state under whose laws it is registered, without losing its corporate identity. This differs from a company incorporating a subsidiary in a foreign country or setting up a branch abroad and transferring all assets and liabilities of one company to another legal entity. The latter is also used as an alternative to the cross-border transfer of the legal seat of a company.

A controversial issue in international private law is whether and to what extent a company can transfer its registered office to another state without the need for liquidation and subsequent re-establishment. In other words, it is a question of a change of the *"company statute"*, which is the law applicable to the company.

In the EU the discussion about the admissibility of a transfer of the seat of companies has been a challenging process, with many decisions of the European Court of Justice (ECJ) and interpretations of the articles 49 and of the Treaty on the Functioning of the European Union. The latest act was the enactment of the Directive 2019/2121 of the European Parliament and of the Council from November 27, 2019 (also known as the *"mobility directive"*) amending the Directive 2017/1132 regarding cross-border conversions, mergers and divisions as a reaction to the newest developments in the caselaw, especially the so-called *"Polbud-Case"* (C-106/16), which opened literally the doors for a better corporate mobility in the EU as it held that the freedom of establishment in the EU also includes the right to change into a legal form of another EU country without having to dissolve the company in the country of origin. The aforementioned Directive entered into force on January 1, 2020 and had to be implemented into national law by January 31, 2023. One of the main new legal concepts brought by this Directive, as a reaction to the *"Polbud-Case"*, is the implementation of the *"cross-border conversion"* of companies, which is defined as being *"an operation whereby a company, without being dissolved or wound up or going into liquidation, converts the legal form under which it is registered in a departure Member State into a legal form of the destination Member State, ..., and transfers at least its registered office to the destination Member State, while retaining its legal personality"* (article 86*b* (2) of the EU Directive 2019/2121). Looking at this definition of conversion it becomes clear that it also entails a transfer of the legal seat of a company from one state to another, but without losing its legal personality and all the assets and liabilities are *"transferred"* to the new entity.[35]

A brief overview of the evolution of the transfer of seat of a company in the case law of the ECJ[36]

The Queen v Treasury and Commissioners of Inland Revenue, ex parte Daily Mail and General Trust PLC (ECJ case C-81/87 of September 27, 1988)

The ECJ established the principle of the free transfer of the registered office, without the company losing *"the legal personality which it enjoys in the legal system of the Member State of incorporation and, where appropriate, the*

---

[35] CHARLOTTE ENE, The Cross-Border Conversion-A Possible Solution for the Mobility of Companies in European Union, Perspectives of Law and Public Administration, 9(1) (2020), p. 56; GITTE SOEGAARD, Cross-border Transfer and Change of Lex Societatis After Polbud, C-106/16: Old Companies Do Not Die... They Simply Fade Away to Another Country, European Company Law, 15(1) (2018), pp. 21 et seq. and OVIDIU IOAN DUMITRU, op. cit., pp. 917 et seq.

[36] Cf. also NICOLA DE LUCA, European Company Law, 2nd edition (2021), p. 131 et seq.

terms of that transfer are determined by the national law under which the company was incorporated".

Judgement of the Court (Grand Chamber) re CARTESIO Oktató és Szolgáltató bt.
(ECJ Case C-210/06 of December 8, 2008)

The ECJ decided in this case that a company incorporated under the law of a member state is not allowed to transfer its seat to another member state while continuing to be registered in the first member state. However, the ECJ held that a company registered in a member state has the right to transfer its seat to another member state if the company will be converted into a company governed under the law of the other member state.

In plain words, the ECJ stated the following:

(i)   The member state of incorporation can prevent a company from transferring its seat to another member state of the EU.

(ii) On the other hand, the freedom of establishment enables a company to move to another member state by converting itself into a form of company governed by the law of that state, without having to be wound up or enter into liquidation during its conversion, if the law of the host member state so permits.

Judgment of the Court (Grand Chamber) re Polbud - Wykonawstwo sp. z o.o.
(ECJ Case C-106/16 of October 25, 2017)

Wykonawstwo sp. z o.o. ('Polbud') was a private limited liability company incorporated under Polish law and established in Łącko. In September 2011, its shareholders decided to transfer the 'company's seat' to Luxembourg, change its name, but keep the legal personality of the company. The company was registered in the Luxembourg Companies Register in 2013 and, as a consequence, it requested the removal from the Polish Trade Registry, but the application was rejected. Polbud reacted and filed a final appeal at the Supreme Court of Poland, claiming that on the day of transfer to Luxembourg, it had changed its legal status and transformed from a Polish company to one under the Luxembourg law. The ECJ was asked, by reference for preliminary ruling, to answer if there was any infringement of the freedom of establishment, so it decided that a situation in which a company created in accordance with the law of a member state wants to convert itself into another company from another member state, with the condition that the entering state checks the existence of the connecting factors, falls within the scope of freedom of establishment, even though that company conducts its main, if not entire, business in the first member state.[37] Moreover, the court noticed that the Polish law states that a company may transfer to another state without losing its legal personality and remove its registration from the national registry, but only if it has been liquidated before and by requiring this, it impedes the cross-border conversion of the company representing a restriction on freedom of establishment.[38]

All member states have now their own set of rules in their national laws about which documents have to be filed in their respective states to their business registries etc. However, there are still significant uncertainties regarding the process, the detailed requirements and the timeline. These issues have to be clarified for each member states.

Cross-border transfer of the seat of a company / cross-border conversions	
Advantages	Disadvantages
Ensures the continuing legal identity of the relocating company and avoids the effort of transferring assets and liabilities between legal entities	Entails an uncertainty regarding its legal requirements, procedure and timeline in each member state
Avoids the burden of dissolving and liquidating the initial legal entity	Can be potentially time-consuming or difficult to plan precisely due to said uncertainty

---

[37] ALEKSANDERS FILLERS, Free Movement of Companies After the Polbud Case, European Business Organization Law Review, 21 (2020), pp. 573-575.
[38] DE LUCA, op. cit., p. 130.

6.2. Transfer of the company from abroad to Switzerland

According to the Swiss legal interpretation, a cross-border transfer of the legal seat of a company while maintaining the company as such is only possible if both the old and the new *"company statute"* agree to such a change. The change of the company statute is to be distinguished from the cross-border transfer of the administrative seat: The latter is permissible without further ado according to the *"incorporation theory"*. Consequently, no liquidation and new formation are required, since the *"company statute"* is not affected by the transfer.

Private international law regulates in article 161 PILA the change from the foreign to the Swiss *"company statute"*. According to para. 1, such an immigration is possible without liquidation and re-incorporation if the foreign law permits it, the company fulfills the change requirements of the foreign law and the adaptation to the Swiss law is possible. By entering into the Swiss *"company statute"*, the foreign entity must correspond to one of the possible company forms of the Swiss *numerus clausus* in corporate law.[39]

Exceptionally, an incorporation in Switzerland can take place without taking into account the foreign company statute if this is approved by the Federal Council (article 161 (2) PILA). In particular, the Federal Council may allow it if *"substantial Swiss interests"* require it. This means exclusively overall interests and not particular interests. The legislator has in mind, for example, a transfer of domicile due to the threat of a nationalization of the company abroad.

Article 162 PILA then regulates the relevant point in time for the change of the *"company statute"*. According to para. 1, a company subject to registration under domestic law becomes subject to Swiss law as soon as it proves that it has transferred the center of its business activities to Switzerland and has adapted to Swiss law. This is intended

---

[39] Cf. EDGAR PHILIPPIN/MATHIEU CHÂTELAIN, Fusioni, scissioni, trasferimenti di patrimonio e di sede transfrontalieri, in: Aspetti patrimoniali e di esecuzione forzata nei rapporti transfrontalieri (2015), pp. 9 et seq.

to prevent Switzerland from being chosen as a mere state of incorporation without other domestic relations being present. If the company is not subject to registration, it is already subject to Swiss law if the intention to do so is clearly recognizable, there is a sufficient relationship with Switzerland and the adaptation to the domestic company statute has taken place. Finally, Article 162 (3) PILA requires companies to prove that their share capital is covered by a report of a licensed auditing expert within the meaning of the Swiss Auditing Supervision Act before registration in one of the Swiss business registries.

6.3. Transfer of the Company from Switzerland to a Foreign Country

In order for a Swiss company to be able to carry out an incorporation into a foreign *"company statute"* (emigration) without liquidation and new formation, the following requirements have to be fulfilled: The company must meet the requirements of Swiss law and continue to exist under the foreign law (article 163 (1) PILA). Then, according to article 163 (2) PILA, a call of debts must be made with reference to the change in the articles of association.

Article 163 PILA does not distinguish between registered and unregistered domestic companies. It follows that the stated requirements apply to all types of companies.

7. Cross-border mergers and demergers

7.1. Generally

Nowadays, probably in most states cross-border mergers and demergers are known. For example, in the EU, there has been a unification of the law based on an old EU regulation of October 9, 1978.[40] Given the significantly increased

---

[40] Third Council Directive 78/855/EEC of October 9, 1978 based on article 54 (3) (g) of the Treaty concerning mergers of public limited liability companies, which is no longer in force. Cf. also HECKSCHEN, op. cit., p. 114.

number of cross-border mergers within the EU and the European Economic Area (EEA) over the past few years, the EU created several directives in this regard: Directive (EU) 2019/2121 of November 27, 2019 (*"Mobility Directive"*) was published on December 12, 2019 and came into force on January 1, 2020. Among other things, it amends the parts of the Directive (EU) 2017/1132 of June 14, 2017 (also known as the *"Codification Directive"*) relating to cross-border mergers, demergers and conversions.[41] According to Article 3 of the Mobility Directive, member states had to bring into force the laws, regulations and administrative provisions that are required to comply with the Directive by January 31, 2023. Until the entry into force of the *"Mobility Directive"*, the *"Codification Directive"* only contained rules on cross-border mergers. Intra-EU cross-border mergers are those mergers where the companies involved are limited liability companies incorporated in accordance with the law

---

[41] The *"Codification Directive"* brings together the provisions of several directives and repeals them in the interests of organization and clarity: (i) Council Directive 82/891/EEC of December 17, 1982, concerning the division of public limited liability companies (6th Directive); (ii) Council Directive 89/666/EC of December 21, 1989, concerning disclosure requirements in respect of branches opened in a member state by certain types of company governed by the law of another State (11th Directive); (iii) Directive 2005/56/EC of the European Parliament and of the Council of October 26, 2005 on cross-border mergers of limited liability companies; (iv) Directive 2009/101/EC of the European Parliament and of the Council of September 16, 2009 on coordination of safeguards which, for the protection of the interests of shareholders and third parties, are required by member states of companies within the meaning of the second paragraph of Article 48 of the Treaty, with a view to making such safeguards equivalent throughout the EU (13th Directive); (iv) Directive 2011/35/EU of the European Parliament and of the Council of April 5, 2011 on mergers of public limited liability companies; and (v) Directive 2012/30/EU of the Parliament and of the Council of October 25, 2012 on coordination of safeguards which, for the protection of the interests of shareholders and others, are required by member states of companies within the meaning of the second paragraph of Article 54 of the Treaty on the Functioning of the European Union, in respect of the formation of public limited liability companies and the maintenance and alteration of their capital, with a view to making such safeguards equivalent throughout the EU.

of two or more states that are part of the EEA, whose registered offices, central administration or principal center of activity are located within the EEA. Other cross-border operations, such as cross-border demergers and conversions, were excluded from its scope of application; the *"Mobility Directive"* has now set forth rules on these transactions and amended the rules on cross-border mergers. One of the main objectives of the changes introduced by the *"Mobility Directive"* was to ensure that the rights and interests of all stakeholders concerned in a cross-border merger process – in particular shareholders, creditors and employees – are protected and duly taken into account.

In Switzerland as a non-EU member state, cross-border mergers and demergers are standardized since the entry into force of the Swiss Merger Act on January 1, 2004 and the PILA was amended accordingly. The relevant law provisions can be found in the articles 163*a*-163*d* PILA. Until their insertion into the law, there were no articles on structural changes of companies in international relations.

7.2. Merger

In a merger, the target company (also called the *"transferor"*) transfers any and all of its assets and liabilities to another company (also called *"transferee"*) with the result of the transferor dissolving without liquidation. The transfer of assets and liabilites is performed by operation of law and leading to a universal succession. Already since the enactment of the EU merger directive and its subsequent transposition into national law, certain companies within the EU were able to merge across jurisdictions.

For example, there are the following types of cross-border mergers which can be pursued by the parties:

- *Merger by absorption*: The target company is *"absorbed"* by transferring all of its assets and liabilities to the transferee company. The transferor is then dissolved without going into liquidation. Such a merger is also called *"general merger"*. If a merger by absorption happens between subsidiaries of a holding company, then such a transaction is called *"side-stream merger"*.

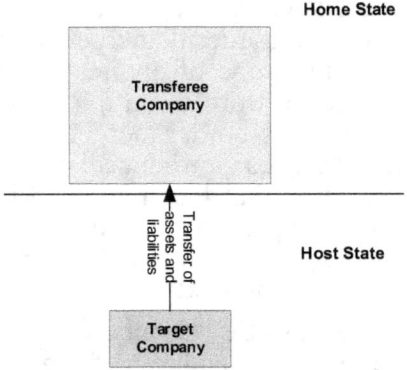

- *Merger by absorption between the holding company and a wholly-owned subsidiary*: Merging a subsidiary into its holding company is referred to as an *"upstream merger"* with the reverse being referred to as *"downstream merger"*. For example, in an *"upstream merger"* the target is a wholly-owned subsidiary of the holding company, which is the transferee, the target is dissolved and upon dissolution the targets assets and liabilities transfer upwards to the transferee.

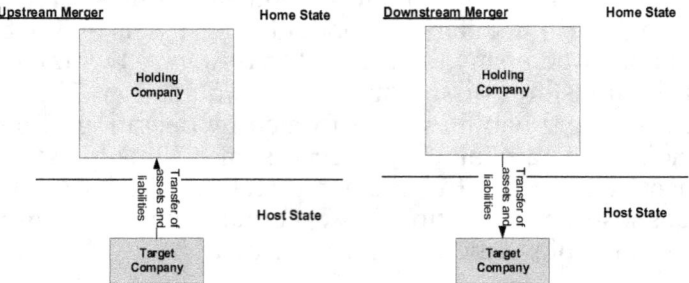

- *Merger by formation of a new company*: Two or more companies (the transferors) each transfer all of their assets and liabilities to a newly-formed 3rd company (the transferee). Once the transfer is complete, the two transferor companies are dissolved without going into liquidation.

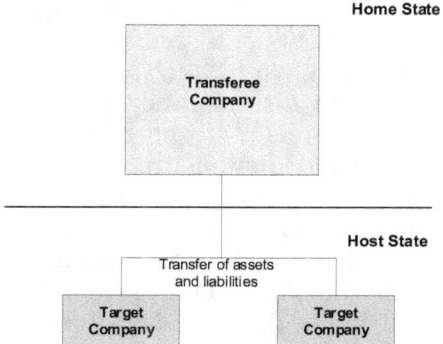

The stages of a merger are typically the following:
- *Preliminary stage:* This stage involves preparing and adopting the common draft merger terms, a directors' report on the merger and an independent expert's report on the merger, if applicable. The specific law of each merging company (*"lex societatis"*) will govern the minimum legal content and bodies in charge of issuing these documents. However, the common draft merger terms must cover at least the following items: (i) share exchange rate and amount of any cash payment; (ii) advantages or special rights granted or attributed to the shareholders or experts who study the merger plan, as well as to the management, monitoring or control bodies of the merging companies; (iii) the date from which the shareholders will be entitled to participate in profits; (iv) the date for accounting purposes; (v) articles of association of the transferee company; (vi) information on the valuation of assets and liabilities and the date of the merger annual accounts; and (vii) information on the procedures by which any employee participation rights are to be determined. In most EU counties, the common draft merger terms are deposited with the relevant authority unless simplified procedures apply.[42] The directors' reports on the merger are prepared by the management bodies of each merging company. These reports, typically the same report for all merging companies, justify the legal and economic

---

[42] Article 91 of the Directive (EU) 2017/1132 of the European Parliament and of the Council of June 14, 2017 relating to certain aspects of company law (*"Codification Directive"*).

grounds for the merger and the likely effect on employees, shareholders and creditors. The specific law of each merging company ("*lex societatis*") may differ, albeit slightly, as to the required contents of the draft merger terms and directors' reports on the merger. For instance, in some jurisdictions, the share exchange rate must always be set out in the merger terms while in other jurisdictions it is not necessary to do so in some cases, or the date of the merger for accounting purposes determined pursuant to the law of one jurisdiction may be inconsistent with the mandatory rules in another jurisdiction. Formal and timing requirements may also differ; for example, while compulsory in some jurisdictions, others do not require all directors to sign the common draft merger terms. The parties must therefore accommodate the different requirements, typically to comply with the most restrictive or protective rules, although this is not possible in all cases and other ad hoc solutions, ideally agreed upon with the competent authorities, may have to be implemented. Finally, an independent expert's report, which is mandatory unless the simplified procedures apply, must cover both the exchange rate and the methods used for its calculation and the sufficiency of the resulting share capital increases.

— *Decision-making and interim stage:* This is the stage where there are most differences between jurisdictions and careful planning is necessary to avoid bottlenecks. For instance, in some EU jurisdictions, such as Spain, France and the Netherlands, no court or other public authority intervenes during the merger process, which is managed entirely by the merging entities, pursuant to a procedure, compliance with which is supervised, and confirmed by the relevant authority at the end of the process as a requirement for the merger to be valid. In some EU countries like Spain, certain documentation must be made available to shareholders, employees and creditors during the merger process. The general meetings must approve the common terms of the merger by a specific majority and the merger must be announced in an official gazette and newspapers. Creditors may oppose the merger following its announcement. Conversely, in other jurisdictions, such as the UK before

Brexit and Ireland, one or more court hearings must be held to allow the court to supervise certain aspects of the merger process and give leave for it to continue, subject to certain waiting periods during which shareholders, employees and creditors are entitled to inspect the merger documents. In practice, these differences may hinder the continuity of the merger process in the jurisdictions involved. In fact, often steps must be taken in one jurisdiction that are not legally required there but are helpful to comply with the requirements in the other jurisdictions involved, such as additional shareholder approvals of the merger.

- *Enforcement and registration stage:* The last stage of the merger process generally involves the submission of the merger documents, which in some jurisdictions, such as Germany, Austria or Spain, must be notarized, to the competent authorities for each of them to verify that the legal requirements have been met, following which they will issue official certificates. The certificate issued by the competent authority of the transferor must be sent to the competent authority of the transferee so that the latter can confirm that the merger is fully effective. Further, the competent authority of the transferee then issues another certificate attesting that the transferor has been removed from its registries.

Due to the participation of EU business registries in different jurisdictions, waiting periods and so on, a cross-border merger will generally take at least 5-7 months to implement. However, if the employees of the company have the right to participate in the decision-making, the process may take longer.

In Switzerland, the law follows the aforementioned distinction between immigration and emigration by differentiating between the merger from abroad to Switzerland (immigration merger; article 163*a* PILA) and the merger from Switzerland to abroad (emigration merger; article 163*b* PILA).[43]

According to article 163*a* (1) PILA, an immigration merger is permissible if the law applicable to the foreign transferring company so permits and the conditions set forth

---

[43] PHILIPPIN/CHÂTELAIN, op. cit., pp. 21 et seq.

therein are met. Otherwise, the immigration merger is subject to Swiss law (article 163*a* (2) PILA). The merger can be affected – as in the domestic relationship – by means of a takeover of the foreign company by the Swiss company (immigration absorption) or by a merger of the domestic and foreign companies to form a new Swiss company (immigration combination).[44]

In the opposite case, in which a Swiss company wants to merge with a foreign company to form a new entity (emigration combination) or is to be taken over by the latter (emigration absorption), the law of the acquiring foreign company is in principle applicable as the merger statute (article 164*b* (4) PILA). However, the emigration merger is subject to a number of conditions: According to article 164*b* (1) a) and b) PILA, the domestic transferring company has to prove that with the merger all its assets and liabilities are transferred to the foreign company (universal succession) and that the share or membership rights are adequately preserved. Next, it should be ensured that the provisions of Swiss merger law are not undermined. Pursuant to article 164*b* (2) PILA, the Swiss company must comply in particular with all provisions of Swiss law applicable to the transferring company. These are the relevant provisions of the Merger Act as well as the mandatory provisions of Swiss corporate law. Finally, in accordance with article 164*b* (3) PILA, the transferring company has to make a debt call in Switzerland.[45]

Since a merger is regularly based on a merger agreement, a strict distinction must be made between corporate law and contract law issues in the international relationship. The corporate law facts are to be connected to the merger statute according to the criteria mentioned. If, on the other hand, questions arise in the cross-border merger in connection with the merger agreement, the applicable law is to be determined according to the rules of article 163*c* PILA. In this respect, the PILA follows its principles on the "*contract statute*" in that the merger agreement is primarily subject to the law chosen by the parties (article 163*c* (2) sentence 1 PILA). In the absence of a choice of law, the merger

---

[44] KINDLER, op. cit., p. 156.
[45] Cf. KINDLER, op. cit., p. 156.

agreement is objectively governed by the law of the closest connection (article 163*c* (1) sentence 2 PILA). Presumably, this closest connection exists with the state whose legal system the acquiring company is subject to. In the sense of a cumulative special connection, article 163*c* (1) PILA stipulates that the merger agreement must comply with the mandatory company law provisions of the laws applicable to the companies involved. According to the wording of the law, this also includes the formal requirements. Article 163*c* (1) PILA has the consequence that in each case the stricter law applies. Article 124 PILA remains irrelevant in connection with the merger agreement. As a result of the cumulative connection, the agreement will always have to comply at least with the provisions of Swiss Merger Act. Accordingly, it requires the written form and the consent of the general meeting or the shareholders of the companies involved.[46]

7.3. Divisions/Demergers

In the EU, the "*Mobility Directive*" introduced a new legal framework for cross-border divisions. So far, the EU legislation captured only rules on "*domestic*" divisions and its rules were inapplicable to cross-border divisions.[47] Up to the "*Mobility Directive*" the majority of the EU member states did not have rules on cross-border divisions; a cross-border division of a company was either impossible, or the same result was achieved through indirect procedures.[48] Articles 160*a*-160*u* EU-Directive 2017/1132 lay down the rules on cross-border divisions. A cross-border division occurs where at least two of the companies involved in the division are governed by the laws of different member states. In the case of a division transaction, a company transfers all of its assets and liabilities to two or more

---

[46] KINDLER, op. cit., pp. 156-157.
[47] Sixth Council Directive 82/891/EEC of December 17, 1982 based on Article 54 (3) (g) of the Treaty, concerning the division of public limited liability companies, OJ L 378, 31.12.1982, pp. 47–54.
[48] DUBRAVKA AKSAMOVIC, Transfer of Corporate Seat in EU: Recent Developments, in: Athens Journal of Law, Volume 5, Issue 4 (2019), pp. 427-428.

companies in the case of a so-called *"full division"*, or transfer part of its assets and liabilities to one or more companies in the case of a so-called *"partial division"* or *"division by separation"*. In return, the shareholders receive shares in the company.[49] The provisions relating to the procedure of cross-border divisions are largely inspired by the existing framework for cross-border mergers and cross-border conversions. Given the similar risks inherent to cross-border divisions as to cross-border conversions, the structured and multi-layered procedure as proposed for conversion would also be required for divisions. The procedure for cross-border divisions follows closely the one for cross-border conversion. The first step in the procedure is drawing up of the draft terms and external experts report, disclosure of those documents to employees, creditors and shareholders, shareholders' approval at the general assembly, examination of documents by the competent authority of the member state of departure and then of the competent authority of the destination member state. Last step is registration of the company in the destinated member state.[50]

The provisions of the PILA on mergers apply *mutatis mutandis* to the facts of cross-border demergers (article 163*d* (1) sentence 1 PILA). A demerger is subject to the law of the demerging company pursuant to article 163*d* (2) PILA. With regard to the demerger agreement, the provisions of Swiss and foreign law apply cumulatively due to the reference in article 163*d* (1) PILA. In this regard, reference is made here to what has been said about the merger agreement and article 163*c* (1) PILA. The parties are also free to choose the applicable law for the demerger agreement (article 163*d* (3) and article 163*c* (2) PILA). In the absence of a choice-of-law, it is presumed that the law of the dividing company will apply.[51]

---

[49] DE LUCA, op. cit., p. 516.
[50] Cf. DUBRAVKA AKSAMOVIC, op. cit., p. 428.
[51] Cf. also PHILIPPIN/CHÂTELAIN, op. cit., pp. 32 et seq. and KINDLER, op. cit., p. 157.

III. Companies in public international law

1. Generally

If there is a cross-border investment or a business transaction between a sovereign state and a company of another state, then such dealings may also be subject to *public international law*. The latter is a body of rules that consists of conventions and international customs, which bind states *inter alia* in their relations with individuals or legal entities of another state, and is founded on certain underlying principles.[52] For example, states are sovereign in their own territory, every state possesses the capacity to enter into treaties or to conclude international conventions, and no state has to submit to the laws of another (*"pari parim non habet imperium"*).[53] *International investment (protection) law* is one of the most *dynamic areas of public international law*. There are many conventions, international customs, principles and judicial decisions which define obligations.[54]

2. Sources of public international law

2.1. Generally

Article *38 of the Statute of the International Court of Justice (ICJ-Statute)*, which concentrates primarily on the activities of states, can be taken as a starting point for an overview of the four classic sources of public international law. This article is widely recognized as an exemplary statement of the aforesaid sources:[55]

---

[52] RICHARD SCHAFFER/FILIBERTO AGUSTI/LUCIEN J. DHOOGE, International business law and its environment (2018), p. 30.
[53] JOHN WARREN HEAD/DAVID FRISCH, Global business law: principles and practice of international commerce and investment (2007), p. 563.
[54] FREYA BAETENS, Investment law within international law: integrationist perspectives (2013), p. xxvii.
[55] Cf. HUGH THIRLWAY, International law and its sources (2014), p. 6; DUNCAN B. HOLLIS, Sources in interpretation theories, in: The Oxford handbook on the sources of international law, edited by Jean D'Aspremont/Samantha Besson/Séverine Knuchel (2017), p. 429

> **Article 38 Statute of the International Court of Justice (ICJ-Statute)**
>
> The Court, whose function is to decide in accordance with international law such disputes as are submitted to it, shall apply:
> 1. international *conventions*, whether general or particular, establishing rules expressly recognized by the contesting states;
> 2. international *custom*, as evidence of a general practice accepted as law;
> 3. the general *principles* of law recognized by civilized nations;
> 4. subject to the provisions of Article 59, *judicial decisions* and the *teachings of the most highly qualified publicists of the various nations*, as subsidiary means for the determination of rules of law.

2.2. Conventions

Article 38(1)(a) of the ICJ-Statute gives priority to *conventions* as a *major feature of international law*.[56] A convention is somehow similar to a contract of private law (where the parties are private persons, while here the parties are sovereign states), which also imposes obligations, and is therefore an international agreement concluded between states in writing, based on their consent to be bound by it and governed by international law. Such agreements are means of creating international rules or standards that states and other actors of the international community are supposed to abide by. These agreements are also referred to as treaties, charters, covenants, declarations, general acts, pacts and statutes, but regardless the various terminologies the substance is the same.[57] There are two types of

---

and MARTIN DIXON, Textbook on international law (2013), pp. 24-25. Article 38 ICJ-Statute does not contain a complete list of the sources of public international law (e.g., there is for example no reference to the UN resolutions).
[56] THIRLWAY, op. cit., p. 7.
[57] This is in line with basic legal principles like *"falsa nominatio non*

conventions: (i) *bilateral conventions*, where only two contracting states are convention partners and bound by it, and (ii) *multilateral conventions*, where a lot of states are signatories and parties to the convention.[58] However, the national law of each signatory state stipulates how a state can become a convention partner. National (constitutional) law provides for the hierarchy of international agreements within the national legal system. In addition, depending on the national law, some act of a national legislation may be required for an international agreement to be given legal effect in the national legal system (e.g., ratification of an international agreement, i.e., its approval by the national parliament).[59]

Very often multilateral conventions allow the signatory states to make reservations or to opt out of certain provisions. Thus, it is possible that a state becomes a party of a convention without acceptation of every provision of it. However, there is a controversy whether a state can make a reservation or objection with regard to specific provisions of a convention if the latter does not offer such a possibility. Nevertheless, it is not possible to make unilaterally a reservation or an objection to a provision after a state has already signed a convention.[60]

As international investment conventions are part of the international law they need to be construed and applied with reference to general rules and concepts of international law. Therefore, it is often referred to the Vienna Convention on the Law of Treaties (VCLT) as its content is the guideline for interpreting and applying international conventions.[61]

---

nocet".

[58] Cf. SCHAFFER/AUGUSTI/DHOOGE, op. cit., p. 30 and DIXON, op. cit., p. 28.
[59] The terms that describe a state's approach to the relationship between the national and international law are monism (national and international law make a unified legal system) and dualism (international agreements have to be transposed into national law). Many states have mixed systems, with some features of both monism and of dualism.
[60] Cf. GEORG DAHM/JOST DELBRÜCK/RÜDIGER WOLFRUM, Völkerrecht, volume I/3 (2013), pp. 558 et seq.
[61] Article 31 VCLT; cf. also HOLLIS, op. cit., p. 429 and TARCISIO GAZZINI, Interpretation of international investment treaties (2016),

The latter governs the international law on treaties between states and as such it is a codification of customary international law.[62] The convention was adopted on May 22, 1969 and opened for signature on May 23, 1969. It entered into force on January 27, 1980 and up to now, 116 states have ratified it. For those states which have not ratified the VCLT, like the United States, the content of this convention is still of the nature of customary rules of international law and they are bound by such customary law.[63]

Furthermore, it is noteworthy that there are many international agreements on trade and investment protections laws such as the WTO agreements, regional or bilateral free trade agreements and other treaties on economic integration (e.g., EU Treaties, NAFTA Agreement, MERCOSUR Agreement), treaties on investment protection like the ICSID-Convention, the Energy Charter Treaty (ECT), the Bretton Woods Agreement on the International Monetary Fund (IMF Statute) and the International Bank for Reconstruction and Development (IBRD).

2.3. International custom

Article 38(1)(b) of the ICJ-Statute mentions that international custom is also a source of public international law. In general, *customary international law* evolved from the consistent *practice or customs of states* is accepted as law.[64] State practices are any act or statement like physical acts, claims, declarations *in abstracto* (e.g., UN General Assembly Resolutions), national laws, national judgments and omissions.[65] It is agreed that the existence of a rule of customary international law requires the presence of two elements: (i) *state practice*, which is uniform, consistent and general (objective element) and (ii) *opinio juris* (subjective

---

pp. 56 et seq.
[62] Cf. CHANG-FA LO, Treaty interpretation under the Vienna Convention on the Law of Treaties (2017), pp. 34 et seq.
[63] CHANG-FA LO, op. cit., p. 33 and DIXON, op. cit., p. 29.
[64] Cf. DIXON, op. cit., p. 32.
[65] J. CRAIG BAKER, International law and international relations, (2000), pp. 56-57. and JOHN YOO/IVANA STRADNER, Customary law today, edited by Laurent Mayali/Pierre Mousseron (2018), p. 320.

element), which is the belief that a practice is compulsory.[66] This is especially the case if a number of states follow the same practice. Furthermore, customary international law can also be created by the practice of international organizations and by the practice of individuals.[67]

In principle, customary international law steps behind specific rules or conventions. However, there is the exception of customary international law rising to the level of *jus cogens* through acceptance by the international community as non-derogable rights (e.g., elementary human rights). No derogation is ever allowed to *jus cogens* as these norms have their roots in natural law principles.[68]

There are various rules of customary international law that might be important in cross border transactions like state responsibility, state immunity and '*minimum standard*' for the treatment of foreign nationals.

2.4. General principles

Article 38(1)(c) of the ICJ-Statute lists the general principles of law recognized by civilized nations as one of the sources of public international law. They play a lesser role as they complement conventions and customary international law.[69] Essentially, they fill the gap if there is neither a provision in an international convention, nor a recognized customary principle of international law available in an investment dispute.[70] These general principles are considered – due to

---

[66] E.g., ICJ, Reports of judgments, advisory opinions and orders, case concerning the continental shelf, North Sea continental shelf cases (Federal Republic of Germany/Denmark; Federal Republic of Germany/Netherlands), Judgment of February 20, 1969, pp. 38 et seq. or ICJ, Reports of judgments, advisory opinions and orders, case concerning the continental shelf (Libyan Arab Jamahiriya/ Malta), Judgment of June 3, 1985, pp. 20-21.

[67] MICHAEL AKEHURST, Custom as a source of international law, British Year Book of International Law (1976), p. 11.

[68] Cf. BRIAN D. LEPARD, Customary international law, a new theory with practical applications (2010), pp. 336-337.

[69] THIRLWAY, op. cit., p. 8.

[70] Cf. JAMES EGERTON-VERNON, Is investment treaty arbitration a mechanism to second-guess governments' exercise of administrative

their level of generality – to be fundamental, as they are widely recognized by states and therefore are common to nearly all legal systems.[71] For example, the principle of good faith is one of these general principles.

2.5. Judicial decisions

Article 38(1)(d) of the ICJ-Statute mentions with regard to judicial decisions that they are *"subsidiary means for the determination of the rules"*. However, although judicial decisions are supposed to be limited to the parties and the particular case, most courts strive to follow previous rulings (*stare decisis*) and on occasion make new international law.[72]

2.6 Teachings of the most highly qualified publicists of the various nations

Article 38(1)(d) of the ICJ-Statute states that the *"teachings of the most highly qualified publicists of the various nations"* are also among the *"subsidiary means for the determination of the rules of law"*. Therefore, the opinions of publicists are on the same level as judicial decisions and thus also considered as subsidiary source of law.[73] However, the teachings of publicists are essential for making the provisions in conventions and creating customary international law as well as general principles of law.

3. Historical background of foreign investment law

In the past oversea investments went to colonies. As the colonies were controlled by imperial states, there was very often no need to develop a comprehensive framework to protect the rights of the investors that were domiciled in the

---

discretion: public law or lex investoria?, in: Investment treaty arbitration and international law, edited by Ian A. Laird, Borzu Sabahi/Frédéric G. Sourgens/Todd J. Weiler (2015), p. 228.
[71] DIXON, op. cit., pp. 43-44.
[72] LINDA A. MALONE, International law (2008), p. 26.
[73] THIRLWAY, op. cit., p. 8.

imperial state. However, if needed the traditional *principle of state responsibility* was applied when states were held responsible for breaches of their obligations under international public law with regard to cross border investments. In the de-colonization-period, which started mainly after the Second World War, the imperial states lost their colonies. The latter became independent and nationalizations became frequent. The purpose of nationalizations was not only economic (to take ownership of previously private investments by foreign parties and transforming them into public assets of newly independent states), but also political (to show the political power and authority of new non-colonial legal orders). There was a pressure for alternatives. The imperial powers saw a need to create new rules in order to protect foreign investments[74] as domestic law was inadequate to protect such investments. In addition to this, there have been conflicts between the USA and Latin America as well as political developments in Eastern Europe, which also led to nationalizations. These events increased the worries that foreign investments were not appropriately protected. The limited influence of a single state, the complexity of economic relations, the fast-changing political situations in states and the activities of transnational companies have fostered the conclusion of conventions in order to create foreign investment laws, the creation of international organizations like the World Bank and other forms of intergovernmental cooperation. However, the principle of state responsibility, which was for a long time nearly the only way to protect investments abroad, has not been replaced and can still be pursued.

4. State responsibility

4.1. Generally

Under the principle of state responsibility, which is considered to be customary international law and a fundamental principle of public international law, states are

---

[74] The first bilateral investment treaty was adopted in 1959 between Germany and Pakistan, entered into force in 1962 and is still in force (cf. http://investmentpolicyhub.unctad.org/IIA/treaty/1732).

generally responsible for breaches of their obligations under international law.[75] Thus, if a state is responsible for a violation of international public law (e.g., through a breach of an obligation in a treaty by a state or when a harm has been done to a foreign company due to an expropriation), then it has to make reparations for such a violation (e.g., compensation for the loss of property). State responsibility covers not only unlawful acts or omissions committed directly by the state, by its member states or provinces, but also acts or omissions of agencies of the state or of individuals if their behavior can be attributed to the state. In such a case, the agency has to act in its official capacity or by authority from the state, respectively the individuals were acting on behalf of the state.[76] In disputes regarding foreign investments it is not easy to enforce the rights of an investor, who is either an individual or a company, as it is not only required that international law must be violated, but also due to the concept of state responsibility, which stipulates that the state has to intervene on behalf of the investor. Still today, as a general rule, an individual or a company has no standing before international tribunals. For example, only states may appear before the ICJ in proceedings. An individual or a company always need specific arrangements by way of specialized treaties setting up appropriate bodies of adjudication.[77]

Mavrommatis Palestine Concessions

Publications of the permanent Court of International Justice, File E.c. III, Docket V.I, Judgment No. 2, August 30, 1924

The case was brought against Great Britain by Greece, because of Great Britain's refusal to recognize, as the sovereign power in Palestine under a mandate assigned by the League of Nations, the contractual rights acquired by

---

[75] Cf. Publications of the permanent court of international justice, Series A., No. 9, July 26, 1927, Case concerning the factory at Chorzów.
[76] Cf. MALONE, op. cit., pp. 47-48.
[77] CHRISTIAN TOMUSCHAT, Individual reparation claims in instances of grave human rights violations: the position under general international law, in: State responsibility and the individual, edited by Albrecht Randelzhofer/Christian Tomuschat (1999), p. 14.

Mavrommatis, a Greek national, through agreements signed with the authorities of the Ottoman Empire, the former sovereign power in Palestine.

The ICJ held: *"...it is true that the dispute was at first between a private person and a State – i.e., between M. Mavrommatis and Great Britain. Subsequently, the Greek Government took up the case. The dispute then entered upon a new phase; it entered the domain of international law, and became a dispute between two States... It is an elementary principle of international law that a State is entitled to protect its subjects, when injured by acts contrary to international law committed by another State, from whom they have been unable to obtain satisfaction through the ordinary channels. By taking up the case of one of its subjects and by resorting to diplomatic action or international judicial proceedings on his behalf, a State is in reality asserting its own rights - its right to ensure, in the person of its subjects, respect for the rules of international law. The question, therefore, whether the present dispute originates in an injury to a private interest, which in point of fact is the case in many international disputes, is irrelevant from this standpoint. Once a State has taken up a case on behalf of one of its subjects before an international tribunal, in the eyes of the latter the State is sole claimant. The fact that Great Britain and Greece are the opposing Parties to the dispute arising out of the Mavrommatis concessions is sufficient to make it a dispute between two States within the meaning of Article 26 of the Palestine Mandate."*

However, before a state can bring a claim to an international tribunal on behalf of an investor, international public law requires that there must be a *link* (e.g., nationality) between the state that starts the procedure and the investor.[78] Though, international public law generally does regulate the relationship between a state and its own citizens, but also holds a state responsible for mistreatment of a citizen of another state. The idea behind this is, that there is a difference between the way a foreigner and the way a citizen

---

[78] Cf. International Court of Justice, Reports of Judgments, advisory opinions and orders, Nottebohm Case (Liechtenstein v. Guatemala), Second Phase, Judgement of April 6, 1955.

is treated. In fact, states have gone to the ICJ and sued other states based on things that have happened to their citizens. One thing that flows from state responsibility is that a state is entitled to diplomatic protection of its individuals.[79] However, opposed to these ideas is the so-called *"Calvo Doctrine"*, named after the Argentine jurist Carlos Calvo, which has been applied throughout Latin America and other areas of the world. This doctrine proposed to prohibit diplomatic protection of a foreigner as he has to be treated like a citizen and thus, he has to use local courts until *"local resources"* were exhausted.[80]

4.2. Individuals

Under international public law, a state may intervene only on behalf of individuals who are their citizens.[81] It is important that the state has a *sufficient link/genuine connection* to the individual before it can make a claim on behalf of the individual.

> **Nottebohm (Liechtenstein v. Guatemala)**
>
> International Court of Justice, Reports of Judgments, advisory opinions and orders, Nottebohm Case (Liechtenstein v. Guatemala), Second Phase, Judgment of April 6, 1955
>
> The ICJ decided that Guatemala was not required to recognize the claim of Liechtenstein to represent Mr. Nottebohm, a naturalized Liechtenstein citizen, who had lived in Guatemala for years and who had very few ties to Liechtenstein, when Liechtenstein claimed that Guatemala had mistreated Mr. Nottebohm. The latter had insufficient links to Liechtenstein.
>
> The term *'nationality'* was understood and defined by the ICJ as a *"legal bond having on its basis a social fact of*

---

[79] Cf. ASTRID KJELDGAARD-PEDERSEN, The international legal personality of the individual (2018), pp. 63-64.
[80] EDUARDO JIMÉNEZ DE ARÉCHAGA, Interview: November 1993, in: Five Masters of International Law (2011), p. 107
[81] Cf. KJELDGAARD-PEDERSEN, op. cit., pp. 63-64.

attachment, a genuine connection of existence, interests and sentiments, together with the existence of reciprocal rights and duties. It may be said to constitute the juridical expression of the fact that the individual upon whom it is conferred, either directly by the law or as the result of an act of the authorities, is in fact more closely connected with the population of the State conferring nationality than with that of any other State. Conferred by a State, it only entitles that State to exercise protection vis-à-vis another State, if it constitutes a translation into juridical terms of the individual's connection with the State which has made him its national."

4.3. Companies

A company has the nationality of the state under the laws of which it was created or incorporated. However, it has been the practice of some states to give a company, created or incorporated under their law, only diplomatic protection when it has its seat, management or center of control in their territory.[82] Thus, there must be a *sufficient link* between the company and the state in order that the latter can bring forward a claim on behalf of the legal entity.

> **Barcelona Traction, Light and Power Company**
>
> International Court of Justice, Reports of Judgments, Advisory Opinions and Orders, Case Concerning The Barcelona Traction, Light and Power Company, Limited (New Application: 1962) (Belgium v. Spain), Second Phase, Judgment of February 5, 1970
>
> The Barcelona Traction, Light and Power Co. was incorporated in 1911 under Canadian law for the purpose of supplying electricity in Spain. In 1938, Spain declared the company bankrupt and took other actions detrimental to it and its shareholders. Canada did not bring a suit in the ICJ,

---

[82] KATE PARLETT, Diplomatic protection and the International Court of Justice, in: The development of international law by the international court of justice, edited by Christian J. Tams/James Sloan (2013), p. 99.

but, since an alleged 88 percent of the shareholders were Belgians, Belgium did. Spain objected that Belgium could not sponsor a complaint on behalf of Barcelona Traction's owners because only the corporation had been injured and the corporation was not Belgian.

The ICJ found that the injured party was the company and not its owners. Therefore, Belgium could not bring a suit to the ICJ against Spain on behalf of the company's Belgian owners. The ICJ noted that Spain had made no objection to Canada bringing a complaint if it chose to do so: *"The Canadian Government's right of protection in respect of the Barcelona Traction company remains unaffected by the present proceedings. The Spanish Government has never challenged the Canadian nationality of the company, either in the diplomatic correspondence with the Canadian Government or before the Court. Moreover, it has unreservedly recognized Canada as the national State of Barcelona Traction in both written pleadings and oral statements made in the course of the present proceedings. Consequently, the Court considers that the Spanish Government has not questioned Canada's right to protect the company."* Thus, only Canada would have been able to sue as the company was registered in Canada.

5. Foreign investment and investment laws

5.1. Definition of foreign investment

5.1.1. Generally

A foreign investment can be defined as any transfer of capital, goods, technology, intellectual property, managerial skills and/or services by an individual or a company of one state to the host state in order to generate wealth.[83]

---

[83] Cf. VALENTINE NDE FRU, The international law on foreign investments and host economies in Sub Saharan Africa, Cameroon, Nigeria, and Kenya (2010), p. 14; KIYOSHI KOJIMA, Direct foreign investment, A Japanese model of multinational business operations, (2010), p. 134 and MUTHUCUMARASWAMY SORNARAJAH, The international law on foreign investment (2010), p. 8 (cit.

Often national investment laws, conventions or investment contracts between an individual or a company, which are acting as investors, and hosts states define in a very detailed way what a foreign investment is. The meaning is very important as it also describes when an investor can ask for protection of his investment or eventually a compensation from a host state for its acts.[84]

Foreign investments can be subdivided in *"foreign direct investment"* and a *"foreign portfolio investment"*.

5.1.2. Foreign direct investments

Foreign direct investments are investments which have been made in order to obtain a lasting interest in a company which is operating in a host state, and thus it is important for the investor to have the equity ownership, control over the operation, management policy and decisions. Generally, foreign direct investments include the formation of a subsidiary in the host state or an investor shareholding with voting rights of at least 10% in a foreign legal entity.[85] Moreover, control of technology, management, and crucial inputs can result in a *de facto control*.[86]

SORNARAJAH, International law). Some authors argue that the widest definition of an *"investment"* in investment treaties can be found in the Energy Charter Treaty (Art. 1/6); cf. ERIC DE BRABANDERE, The Settlement of Investment Disputes in the Energy Sector, in: Foreign investment in the energy sector, Balancing private and public interests, edited by Eric De Brabandere/Tarcisio Gazzini (2014), p. 14.

[84] Cf. also SORNARAJAH, International law, p. 10.
[85] The voting rights should, generally speaking, give the investor some control over or of the object of the investment.
[86] Cf. HARRISON G. BLAINE, Foreign direct investment (2009), p. vii; MEHDI RASOULI GHAHROUDI/YASUO HOSHINO/STEPHEN JOHN TURNBULL, Foreign direct investment, Ownership advantages, firm specific factors, survival and performance (2018), pp. 1-2 and PETER J. BUCKLEY/GERALD D. NEWBOULD/JANE THURWELL, Foreign direct investment by smaller UK firms: the success and failure of first-time investors abroad (1988), p. 74.

5.1.3. Foreign portfolio investments

A portfolio investment is done by acquiring ownership of financial assets or participations in a company incorporated or acting in another state without the same degree of direct control as in a foreign direct investment.[87] Usually they are short-term in nature.[88] These investments aim only to make profit and do not lead to technology transfer, to training of local cadres or a lasting interest in the investment or effective management control over a legal entity.[89] Portfolio investments involve a high turnover of securities; examples are debt certificates (money market securities, bonds), dividend-paying securities (shares, participation certificates, profit certificates) and mutual fund certificates.[90]

5.1.4. Distinction of the kind of investments

The distinction between these two different kinds of investments is not just theoretical as they are of practical importance. For example, ICSID does not provide protection regarding investment disputes related to portfolio investments.[91]

Main elements for distinguishing foreign direct investments from foreign portfolio investments

Ownership and control over the operation, management policy and decisions of the company and share ownership: A foreign portfolio investment is characterized by a separation between the control over the operation, management policy as well as the decisions and the ownership of the participations of the company. Whereas in

---

[87] Cf. BLAINE, op. cit., p. 26.
[88] GHAHROUDI/HOSHINO/TURNBULL, op. cit., p. 1.
[89] NOAH RUBINS, The notion of 'investment' in international investment arbitration, in: Arbitrating foreign investment disputes, procedural and substantive legal aspects, volume 19, edited by Norbert Horn (2004), p. 317.
[90] Cf. MEHDI RASOULI GHAHROUDI/YASUO HOSHINO/STEPHEN JOHN TURNBULL, op. cit., p. 1.
[91] Cf. SORNARAJAH, International law, pp. 8-9.

a foreign direct investment the investor wants also to have an effective voice in the management of the company.

Long term aspect/withdraw of investment: The investment of a foreign portfolio investor is of short-term in nature, he can easily withdraw his investment or transfer it to another investment. However, a foreign direct investment consists of a long-term commitment in which assets are bound and thus not easy to liquidate.

5.2. Investments laws

5.2.1. Generally

Foreign investments are important for the economic growth and prosperity of states. They are significant for any state, but for instance they have special meaning for developing countries. On one hand, they provide foreign investors with new markets and marketing channels, cheaper production facilities, access to new technology and products.[92] On the other hand, the host state receives new capital, products, technologies and management skills.[93]

Thus, in order that foreign investments are made, there needs to be a legal investment protection, which is not only creating trust, but also reducing the risks of state interference.[94] Such risks derive *inter alia* from expropriation, restrictions on the transfer of assets, sanctions due to non-compliance with the domestic law, denial of permits, or other forms of unfair, inequitable, discriminatory or arbitrary treatment.

The law that applies to foreign investments consists of a complex bundle of (i) domestic investment legislation, (ii) investment treaties (bilateral and multilateral), and (iii) investment contracts between investors and states.

---

[92] SAHID AHMED, Foreign direct investment, trade and economic growth: An introduction, in: Foreign direct investment, trade and economic growth, exploring challenges and opportunities, edited by Sahid Ahmed (2013), p. 3.
[93] Cf. M. MARIA JOHN KENNEDY, International economics (2014), p. 293.
[94] Cf. OECD POLICY FRAMEWORK FOR INVESTMENT (2015), p. 53.

5.2.2. Domestic investment legislation

In order to regulate, attract, promote or facilitate foreign investments, states usually issue *"investment laws"* or *"investment codes"* in their domestic law. In these investment legislations they offer a variety of guarantees, administrative services, tax incentives etc. However, also other fields of law are of importance. Thus, the host states very often amend their company law, commercial law, property law, labor law, civil procedure or criminal law in order to create a favorable environment for foreign investors.[95]

Moreover, certain countries generally allow investments only in the form of joint ventures and thus these countries have specific *"joint venture laws"*. A joint venture guarantees a host state to influence the management of a company, as local participants in the ownership and control of the investment project are involved.[96] Furthermore, a few states have enacted special investment laws that apply to particular sectors of the economy, such as agriculture, technology, tourism, services, or certain manufacturing areas, or their laws have been amended accordingly.[97]

5.2.3. Investment treaties

In the last decades of the 20th century there was not only a striking increase in the flow of investments, but also the countries involved, the economic sectors concerned and the forms of investments evolved greatly.[98] The rise of foreign

---

[95] Cf. ALAN S. GUTTERMAN, The law of domestic and international strategic alliances (1995), p. 146 et seq. and MARIEL DIMSEY, The resolution of international investment disputes, Challenges and solutions (2008), p. 16.
[96] SORNARAJAH, International law, p. 107.
[97] Cf. ALAN S. GUTTERMAN, A short course in international joint ventures, Negotiating, forming and operating the international joint venture (2002), pp. 90-91.
[98] MARTIN ENDICOTT, The definition of investment in ICSID Arbitration: Development lessons for the WTO?, in: Sustainable development in world trade law, edited by Markus W. Gehring/Marie-Claire Cordon (2005), p. 409.

investments created a need for protection of the latter and investors against potentially 'unstable' legal systems of host states and thus led to an increase of investment treaties.[99] However, due to the influence of the aforementioned *"Calvo doctrine"*, which created *inter alia* a resistance towards the internationalization of investment protection, many countries in South America were initially not so keen in entering into investment treaties. Though, especially the United States bilateral treaty program with South America contributed to the demise of the *"Calvo doctrine"* in Latin America.[100] Nowadays, we count more than 3,000 investment treaties, of which two-thirds were concluded in the 1990s.[101] Investment treaties have either the form of bilateral investment or multilateral investment conventions (*"BITs"* and *"MITs"*). The latter have been mainly concluded on a regional and interregional level. These treaties serve as a major vehicle for the protection of foreign investment interests of investors and their home states, but they were also created in order to promote foreign investment.[102]

Most investment treaties are concluded between developed and developing states at the developed state's request. Though, these investment conventions are supposed to be reciprocal, the protection is usually for the benefit of the developed states as the investments are made by its investors. Therefore, the treaty outcome does not always seem to be fair and there is often an inequity stipulated in the treaty. Even though, article 51 of the VCLT provides that where a state's consent to a treaty has been procured by coercion of its representatives through acts or threats directed against them, the treaty will have no legal effect,

---

[99] DIMSEY, op. cit., p. 14.
[100] MAVLUDA SATTOROVA, Reassertion of control and contracting parties' domestic law responses to investment treaty arbitration, between reform, reticence and resistance, in: Reassertion of control over the investment treaty regime, edited by Andreas Kulick (2017), p. 53 and CHRISTOPHER F. DUGAN/DON. WALLACE, JR./NOAH D. RUBINS/BORZU SABAHI, Investor-State arbitration (2011), p. 69.
[101] BURKHARD SCHÖBENER/JOCHEN HERBST/MARKUS PERKAMS, Internationales Wirtschaftsrecht (2010), p. 247 and DIMSEY, op. cit., p. 14.
[102] EVA NIEUWENHUYS/MARCEL BRUS, Legal, political and economic aspects, in: Multilateral regulation of investment, edited by Eva Nieuwenhuys/Marcel Brus (2001), p. 4.

and article 52 VCLT states that the consequence is the same where threat or force has procured agreement to a treaty, there is no acceptance in international law that the mere economic pressure to enter in a treaty constitutes grounds for invalidating the agreement. Moreover, developing countries are not invoking these principles not just because they have no real evidence on this point, but also because they frequently lack the resources required to do so and they fear economic reprisals. However, an unfair behavior does not affect the validity of investment treaties under public international law.[103] On the other hand, it may be argued that an investment that was not made in accordance with the laws of the host state or international law is not protected by the investment legislation in general.[104]

Nevertheless, also some investment treaties were concluded between developing countries.[105] Furthermore, the investment treaties do not only set out the rules for foreign investments, but they are also a very important instrument in terms of creating a favorable investment environment, improved productivity and international competitiveness.[106]

Although it is difficult to make – besides the fact that these BITs and MITs promote investment and protect the interests of foreign investors from actions or omissions of the host state – general statements about the content of investment treaties, the latter usually grant investments made by an investor of one contracting state in the territory of the other the following guarantees:[107]

- Obligation of the host state to treat investors according to so-called *"minimum international standards"*;[108]

---

[103] Cf. LAURENCE BOULLE, The law of globalization: an introduction (2009), p. 144.
[104] RUDOLPH DOLZER/CHRISTOPH SCHREUER, Principles of international investment law (2012), pp. 92-93.
[105] DIMSEY, op. cit., p. 13 and ANDREAS F. LOWENFELD, International economic law (2002), p. 456.
[106] INTERNATIONAL MONETARY FUND, Foreign private investment in developing countries (1985), p. 11.
[107] Cf. DIMSEY, op. cit., p. 14.
[108] DESSISLAV DOBREV, Reforming international investments laws: Is it time for a new international social contract to rebalance the investor-state regulatory dichotomy?, in: Yearbook on international investment law & policy 2014 – 2015, edited by Andrea K.

- Rights of investors to freely transfer currency out of the host state;[109]
- Right of the host state to expropriate assets of the investor located in the host state, with a corresponding duty to provide compensation;[110] and
- Settlement of disputes between investors and the host state through international arbitration.[111]

Especially developed states, which are very active in negotiating investment conventions like the United States or Canada, usually have a boiler plate *"model treaty"* that is used as a starting basis for their negotiations with other states. Furthermore, many of the provisions in these *"model treaties"* are based on rules of customary international law.[112]

Nonetheless, in an investment dispute it might be necessary to have a close look at the validity of a certain provision in an investment treaty (e.g., if its content is in conflict with customary international law). Thus, it has to be distinguished whether the provision is an ordinary regulation or it is in contradiction with *jus cogens*. Art. 53 VCLT states that a provision in a treaty that contradicts *jus cogens* is void. The superior normative state of *jus cogens* rules has also been confirmed in several investment awards.[113] Even

---

Bjorklund (2016), p. 275.

[109] JESWALD W. SALACUSE, The law of investment treatises (2009), p. 264.
[110] TILMANN MICHAEL DRALLE, Ownership unbundling and related measures in the EU energy sector, Foundations, the impact of WTO law and investment protection (2018), p. 238 and YI SHIN TANG, The international trade policy for technology transfers: legal and economic dilemmas on multilateralism versus bilateralism (2009), p. 84.
[111] LOWENFELD, op. cit., p. 456 and DIMSEY, op. cit., p. 14.
[112] Cf. LEON E. TRAKMAN/NICOLAS W. RANIERI, Foreign direct investment: a historical perspective, in: Regionalism inter international investment law, edited by Leon E. Trakman/Nicolas W. Ranieri (2013), p. 20.
[113] Cf. MOSHE HIRSCH, Sources of international investment law, international investment law and soft law, edited by Andrea K. Bjorklund/August Reinisch (2012), p. 33 and MOSHE HIRSCH, Interactions between investment and non-investment obligations, The Oxford handbook of international investment law, edited by Peter Muchlinski/Federico Ortino/Christoph Schreuer (2008), p. 157. An example for such an investment award is the following:

though there are states like the United States, which are not party to the VCLT, the previously mentioned rule applies as it is considered as customary international law.

5.3. Investment contracts between investors and states

5.3.1. Generally

An investor may enter into an investment contract with the host state. There are varieties of such contracts, and their subject can be very wide. For example, such contracts are made frequently with regard to the extraction of natural resources (e.g., exploration and exploitation of oil, gas and minerals).[114] These contracts were made in order to protect the investors of unilateral changes by the host state (e.g., due to changes in the domestic law), which affect negatively the investors interests. However, a state's powers within its borders are not limitless under international public law. A host state is usually bound by the promises it made to the investor. Therefore, a breach of such an investment contract is also a breach of international law.

Usually, under the principle of state responsibility investors have no legal personality on the international level; they might have to ask their home states to go forward for them in order to assert their claims. Nevertheless, investors have moved away from the simple diplomatic protection thanks to contractual stipulations in internationalized investment contracts between investors and the host state or BITs or MITs according to which they were able to enforce directly their rights before international tribunals or arbitration and thus they acquired partial legal personality under international law.

Corn Products International, Inc. v. United Mexican States, ICSID Case No. ARB (AF)/04/01, para. 149.

[114] Cf. FEDERICO ORTINO/NIMA MERSADI TABARI, International dispute settlement: The settlement of investment disputes concerning natural resources – applicable law and standards of review, in: Research handbook on international law and natural resources, edited by Elisa Morgera/Kati Kulovesi (2016), p. 515.

5.3.2. Investor-state contracts

A contract between a foreign investor and a host state binds the state under international law when it is *"internationalized"*. Such *"internationalization"* of an investor-state-contract occurs when the contract integrates international standards into the applicable law of their contractual relations by referring to customary international law or to BITs or MITs, which are ratified by their home or host states.[115] For example, the investor is granted by the host state a compensation and a fair and equitable treatment. Furthermore, the parties agree that to the extent that law of the host state governs the contract, it will not be unilaterally modified by the host state. Once a contract is *"internationalized"*, a state is responsible under international law for a breach of the contract. Furthermore, the effect of *"internationalization"* of contracts has been affirmed by international tribunals.[116]

Internationalization is accomplished by the inclusion of an (i) international choice-of-law clause and/or a (ii) *"stabilization clause"* in the investor-state agreement.

5.3.2.1. International-choice-of-law clause

An international-choice-of-law-clause[117] states that the international law will govern the contractual relationship between the parties and the principles of international law will be applied. The purpose of this type of clause is to *"internationalize"* the contract and thus protect it from attempts by the host state to cancel or modify it without the consent of the investor.[118]

---

[115] Cf. MUTHUCUMARASWAMY SORNARAJAH, Resistance and change in the international law on foreign investment (2015), pp. 78 et seq. (cit. SORNARAJAH, Resistance).
[116] Cf. JESWALD W. SALACUSE, The three law of international investment: National, contractual, and international frameworks for foreign capital (2013), p. 390 (cit. SALACUSE, The three laws of international investment).
[117] An international-choice-of-law-clause is not the same as a *"classical"* choice-of-law-clause, which refers solely to the law of a particular jurisdiction.

Example of an international-choice-of-law-clause

The contractual relationship is governed by the principles of law of [state] common to the principles of international law and in the absence of such common principles then by and in accordance with the general principles of law, including such of those principles as may have been applied by international tribunals.

Texaco Overseas Petroleum Company v. The Government of the Libyan Arab Republic
(1977) 53 ILR 389

In this case the tribunal held that one effect of an internationalization of a contract is that the individuals acquire and can enforce certain rights against the state: *"...stating that a contract between a State and a private person falls within the international legal order means that for the purposes of interpretation and performance of the contract, it should be recognized that a private contracting party has specific international capacities. But, unlike a State, the private person has only a limited capacity and his quality as a subject of international law does enable him only to invoke, in the field of international law, the rights which derive from the contract. ... The application of the principles of Libyan law does not have the effect of ruling out the application of the principles of international law, but quite the contrary: it simply requires us to combine the two in verifying the conformity of the first with the second."*

5.3.2.2. Stabilization clause

The stabilization clause states that between the parties of an investor-state-contract, the law of the host state as of the date of the contract or such other date agreed to by the parties governs the contractual relationship. The parties make sure that the applicable law on their contractual relations is safe from subsequent changes of the domestic

---

[118] SALACUSE, The three laws of international investment, p. 319.

law. The stabilization clause literally *"freezes"* the applicable law.[119]

AGIP S.p.A. v. People's Republic of the Congo
ICSID Case No. ARB/77/71
In 1962, AGIP set up a legal entity under the law of the Republic of Congo for oil distribution activities. The legal entity was exempted from the nationalizations in 1974. Art. 11 of the agreement contained a stabilization clause: *"... adopt appropriate measures to prevent the application to the Company of future amendments to company law affecting the structure and composition of Company bodies..."*

5.3.3. Investors rights under investment conventions

Modern BITs and MITs grant to an investor the right to sue a host state directly in international arbitration, if he believes that the BIT or MIT governing his investment has been violated (e.g., Energy Charter Treaty).[120] The ability for a foreign national or a company to sue a host state directly has been described as a revolutionary innovation that has caused a profound transformation of international public law.[121] For such a right to sue the state directly in an international arbitration by the foreign investor, a specific consent has to be given in the convention.[122]

---

[119] SORNARAJAH, Resistance, p. 110.
[120] SCHÖBENER/HERBST/PERKAMS, op. cit., p. 248.
[121] Cf. A. CLAIRE CUTLER, International commercial arbitration, transnational governance, and the new constitutionalism, in: International arbitration & global governance, Contending theories and evidence, edited by Walter Mattli/Thomas Dietz (2014), p. 145 and TRINH HAI YEN, The interpretation of investment treaties (2014), p. 168.
[122] ERIC DE BRABANDERE, Investment treaty arbitration as public international law, procedural aspects and implications (2014), p. 59.

5.4. Binding effect of investor-state contracts and investment treaties

As states can enter into contracts and treaties and convey special rights to investors, there is also the risk that the same states take away these special rights. However, once a state entered into investment contracts and treaties, it is bound to respect its consent expressed in these agreements.

> **Article 26 VCLT "Pacta sunt servanda"**
> *"Every treaty in force is binding upon the parties to it and must be performed by them in good faith."*

The rule *"pacta sunt servanda"* is part of customary international law and a fundamental principle which dates back to early civilizations and became more and more important with the development of international law.[123] It does not only apply to conventions between states, but also governs contracts between investors and states.[124]

> **Sapphire International Petroleum Limited v. National Iranian Oil Company-Case**
> Sapphire Award, ILR 1963, at 136 et seq.
> According to the arbitrators, it has been duly established that one party deliberately refused to carry out certain of its obligations and that this failure is a breach of contract: *"Moreover, it is a fundamental principle of law, which is constantly being proclaimed by international courts, that contractual undertakings must be respected. The rule pacta sunt servanda is the basis of every contractual relationship. Moreover, it is contained in the laws of both parties to the dispute..."*

For example, if a state enters into a contract with an investor of another state, and then breaches the agreement because of changes in the domestic law, there is not only a violation of

---

[123] Cf. KIRSTEN SCHMALENBACH, Art. 26 Pacta sunt servanda, in: Vienna Convention on the Law of Treatises, A commentary, edited by Oliver Dörr/Kirsten Schmalenbach (2012) p. 436.
[124] SALACUSE, The three laws of international investment, p. 319.

the contract, but this is also a breach of public international law.

> **Final ICC Award No. 5485, YCA 1989, at 156 et seq.**
> According to the arbitrators, a specific article of an agreement was clear and had to be applied literally: *"Whereas the rule pacta sunt servanda implies that the contract is the law of the parties, agreed to by them for the regulation of their legal relationship, and generates not only the obligation of each party to a contract to fulfill its promises, but also the obligation to perform them in good faith, to compensate for the damage caused to the other party by their non-fulfillment and to not terminate the contract unilaterally except as provided for in the contract."*

However, there is a risk that a state might try to justify its acts by invoking another principle of public international law that is called *"clausula rebus sic stantibus"*, which allows to terminate an agreement due to a change of circumstances after the conclusion of a contract.

> **Article 62 VCLT *"Fundamental change of circumstances"***
> *"1. A fundamental change of circumstances which has occurred with regard to those existing at the time of the conclusion of a treaty, and which was not foreseen by the parties, may not be invoked as a ground for terminating or withdrawing from the treaty unless:*
> *(a) the existence of those circumstances constituted an essential basis of the consent of the parties to be bound by the treaty; and*
> *(b) the effect of the change is radically to transform the extent of obligations still to be performed under the treaty.*
> *2. A fundamental change of circumstances may not be invoked as a ground for terminating or withdrawing from a treaty:*
> *(a) if the treaty establishes a boundary; or*
> *(b) if the fundamental change is the result of a breach by the party invoking it either of an obligation under the treaty*

or of any other international obligation owed to any other party to the treaty.

3. If, under the foregoing paragraphs, a party may invoke a fundamental change of circumstances as a ground for terminating or withdrawing from a treaty it may also invoke the change as a ground for suspending the operation of the treaty."

In order that the principle *"clausula rebus sic stantibus"* has priority over the principle *"pacta sunt servanda"*, the change in circumstance has to be fundamental in order to be sufficient to disrespect a contractual relationship.

Fisheries Jurisdiction

(United Kingdom of Great Britain and Northern Ireland v. Iceland)

I.C.J., 1973 I.C.J. 3

In this case the ICJ stated that *"... the changes of circumstances which must be regarded as fundamental or vital are those which imperil the existence or vital development of one of the parties."*

Although, parties have often invoked the principle *"clausula rebus sic stantibus"* before the ICJ or other tribunals, the latter mostly refused to apply this principle.

6. Remedies in case of violation of public international law

6.1. Generally

Due to the principle that no state has to submit to the laws of another (*"pari parim non habet imperium"*), an investor will be faced with problems of the *sovereign immunity (state immunity)* of the host state. Sovereign immunity is a principle of customary international law, by virtue of which a sovereign state cannot be sued before the courts of another sovereign state without its consent and thus is exempt from the jurisdiction of foreign national courts.[125]

The Schooner Exchange v. McFaddon
11. U.S. 116, 137 (1812)

The U.S. Supreme Court stated: *"The full and absolute territorial jurisdiction being alike the attribute of every sovereignty and being incapable of conferring extraterritorial power, does not contemplate foreign sovereigns, nor their sovereign rights as its objects. One sovereign can be supposed to enter a foreign territory only under an express license or in the confidence that the immunities belonging to his independent, sovereign station, though not expressly stipulated, are reserved by implication and will be extended to him."*

Until the mid of the twentieth century, there has been mutual respect for the independence, legal equality, and dignity of all states. Thus, there was an *"absolute immunity"*. However, as states entered more and more in trading and various commercial activities, it became clear that such a strict immunity deprived for example investors that entered with a state in such activities of their remedies. Thus, the doctrine of *"restrictive immunity"* was created. According to this doctrine, a state cannot claim sovereign immunity if a lawsuit is based on its commercial activities. Therefore, it is important to distinguish between *"acta jure imperii"*, which are sovereign and also public acts of a state that are usually exempt from assessment or damages awarded by a tribunal of another state, and *"acta jure gestionis"*, which refer to commercial acts for which states cannot claim to be immune in front of the tribunal. However, it is sometimes quite difficult to distinguish these kinds of acts.[126]

Re Canada Labour Code
[1992] 2 SCR 50, 1992 CanLII 54 (SCC)

---

[125] STEPHAN W. SCHILL, The backlash against investment arbitration, edited by Michael Waibel/Asha Kaushal/Kyo-Hwa Liz Chung/Claire Balchin (2010), p. 34.

[126] ERNEST K. BANKAS, The state immunity controversy in international law, private suits against sovereign states in domestic courts (2005), p. 74.

The Supreme Court of Canada stated: *"Historically, states enjoyed an absolute immunity from adjudication by foreign courts. Under international law, it was accepted that sovereign states should not be "embarrassed" by subjection to the control of a foreign judiciary. Over time, however, as governments increasingly entered into the commercial arena, the doctrine of absolute immunity was viewed as an unfair shield for commercial traders operating under the umbrella of state ownership or control. The common law responded by developing a new theory of restrictive immunity. Under this approach, courts extended immunity only to acts jure imperii, and not to acts jure gestionis."*

6.2. Remedies available to the state

6.2.1. Generally

If the acts of a state violate public international law (e.g., expropriation of the property of an investor without compensation by the host state), then the state becomes responsible to another state and the injured state can rely on the following remedies:

– Remedies under customary international law like state responsibility[127] and/or
– Remedies set forth in international investment treaties.[128]

Chorzów Factory

Factory at Chorzow (Germ. v. Pol.), Series A.-No. 17, September 13, 1928, Collection of Judgments, No. 13, Case concerning the factory at Chorzów

In this case the ICJ stated that: *"The essential principle contained in the actual notion of an illegal act – a principle which seems to be established by international practice and in particular by the decisions of arbitral tribunals – is that reparation must, as far as possible, wipe out all the*

---

[127] Cf. R. RAJESH BABU, Remedies under the WTO legal system 2012), pp. 52 et seq. and CHRISTINE D. GRAY, Judicial remedies in international law (1990), p. 210.
[128] Cf. DE BRABANDERE, op. cit., p. 65.

consequences of the illegal act and reestablish the situation which would, in all probability, have existed if that act had not been committed. Restitution in kind, or, if this is not possible, payment of a sum corresponding to the value which a restitution in kind would bear; the award, if need be, of damages for loss sustained which would not be covered by restitution in kind or payment in place of it - such are the principles which should serve to determine the amount of compensation due for an act contrary to international law."

The aforementioned excerpt describes that a state may demand reparation for a wrongful act by the host state in order to wipe out all the consequences of the illegal act.

Reparations in the form of restitution in kind and compensation are predominant in public international law.

6.2.2. Restitution in kind

The host state has to recover as a restitution in kind (*"restitutio in integrum"*) any losses by the return of the same or new goods to the other state. Thus, the injured state is entitled to obtain from the state, which has committed an act according to public international law, the re-establishment of the situation that existed before the wrongful act was committed. However, it is possible to combine the restitution in kind with other remedies.[129]

Temple of Preah Vihear

Reports of Judgments, Advisory opinions and orders, Case concerning the temple of Preah Vihear (Cambodia v. Thailand), Merits, Judgment of June 15, 1962

In 1904, Siam and the French colonial authorities ruling Cambodia formed a joint commission to demarcate their mutual border mainly by following the watershed line of the Dângrêk mountain range, which placed nearly all of the Preah Vihear temple on Thailand's side. The border's location was depicted on a map in 1907 by French officers on which the Preah Vihear area and its temple was placed

---

[129] ANTHONY AUST, Modern treaty law and practice (2000), p. 302.

on the Cambodian side. This map was sent to the Siamese authorities and used in the ruling of the ICJ. After the withdrawal of French troops from Cambodia in 1954, Thai forces occupied the temple. However, Cambodia protested and asked the ICJ to rule that the temple and the surrounding land lay in Cambodian territory.

On June 15, 1962 the ICJ found *"by nine votes to three, ... that the Temple of Preah Vihear is situated in territory under the sovereignty of Cambodia; by nine votes to three, that Thailand is under an obligation to withdraw any military or police forces, or other guards or keepers, stationed by her at the Temple, or in its vicinity on Cambodian territory; by seven votes to five, that Thailand is under an obligation to restore to Cambodia any objects of the kind specified in Cambodia's fifth Submission which may, since the date of the occupation of the Temple by Thailand in 1954, have been removed from the Temple or the Temple area by the Thai authorities."*

6.2.3. Compensation

Compensation is the most likely remedy to be sought by a foreign state, especially when its nationals or companies have suffered a loss from the host state. If damage has been caused by the illegal act, then the injured state has to be placed in the position it would have been if there has not been a wrongful action or omission, and the legal consequences which flow therefrom. The compensation must encompass not only the losses incurred (*damnum emergens*), but also the gains prevented or lost profits (*lucrum cessans*).[130] However, in practice it is unclear, whether the compensation has to be appropriate or full.[131]

---

[130] AUST, op. cit., p. 304 and BORZU SABAHI/NICHOLAS J. BIRCH, Comparative compensation for expropriation, in: International investment law and comparative public law, edited by Stephan W. Schill (2010), p. 768.

[131] Cf. SORNARAJAH, International law, p. 440; SUSAN BREAU, Questions & answers, international law 2013 and 2014 (2014), p. 156.

Corfu Channel

International Court of Justice, Reports of judgments, Advisory opinions and orders, The Corfu Channel Case (Merits), Judgment of April 9, 1949

After several encounters from May 1946 to November 1946 in the Corfu Channel between the United Kingdom and the People's Republic of Albania, not only two Royal Navy ships have been damaged, but there has been also a significant loss of life. Thus, the United Kingdom was seeking for reparations in the ICJ. After an initial ruling on jurisdiction in 1948, the ICJ issued separate merits and compensation judgments in 1949.

In this case the ICJ held: *"If, however, the Court is competent to decide what kind of satisfaction is due to Albania ..., it is difficult to see why it should lack competence to decide the amount of compensation which is due to the United Kingdom ... If, however, the Court should limit itself to saying that there is a duty to pay compensation without deciding what amount of compensation is due, the dispute would not be finally decided... For the foregoing reasons, the Court has arrived at the conclusion that it has jurisdiction to assess the amount of the compensation...."*

Eventually, the ICJ awarded the United Kingdom a compensation of £ 843,947.

Generally, there is the idea, which is also expressed in the *"CHORZÓW FACTORY"-case*, that there is a primacy of restitution in kind and therefore it is considered as the main remedy for all breaches of international law.[132] However, restitution in kind is for example not so often awarded in the jurisprudence of ICJ. Thus, compensation has been by far the most used frequently used remedy in international investment disputes.[133]

---

[132] Cf. ALEXANDER ORAKHELASHVILI, Peremptory norms and reparation for internationally wrongfully acts, in: Baltic Yearbook of international law, Volume 3, edited by Ineta Ziemle, (2003), pp. 35-36. Especially in the context of human rights and humanitarian law, this primacy of restitution becomes more than clear.

[133] Cf. SERGEY RIPINSKY/KEVIN WILLIAMS, Damages in international investment law (2008), pp. 49 et seq.

However, before a lawsuit can be brought to the ICJ, several prerequisites must be met. Among these prerequisites is the so-called principle of *"exhaustion of local effective remedies"*. This principle is required by the ICJ because the latter considers it as well-established international customary law.[134]

6.3. Legal basis for remedies available to the investors

6.3.1. Generally

Traditionally, the principle of state responsibility is only applicable to states. However, as it has been mentioned before, investors from another state can become under certain circumstances the subject to rules of international public law. Thus, the investor can invoke remedies regardless of the fact whether its home state is going to pursue remedies or not. If the acts of a state violate public international law (e.g., breach of a contract between the host state and a foreign investor) and thus that state becomes responsible to an investor, then the injured investor can come forward on the following legal grounds.

6.3.2. Remedies provided in an international agreement

A BIT between the investors' home state and the state responsible for the injury or even a MIT may provide remedies to an injured investor for the wrongful actions or omissions, and the legal consequences which flow therefrom by the host state.[135]

---

[134] Cf. e.g., Interhandel (Switzerland v. USA), ICJ reports 1959, p. 6 and 27; MALCOLM N. SHAW, International law (2017), p. 620 and PHILIPPE COUVREUR, The international court of justice and the effectiveness of international law (2017), p. 253.

[135] BORZU SABAHI, Compensation and restitution in investor-state arbitration, Principles and practice (2011), p. 11. An *"umbrella clause"* is a treaty provision found in many BITs that requires each contracting state to observe all investment obligations it has assumed with respect to investors from the other contracting state. Such a clause can elevate a contract claim to the level of a treaty claim and thus a violation of an investment contract is deemed to be

6.3.3. Remedies provided in the domestic law of the state responsible for the injury

It is possible that the domestic law of the host state provides remedies to an injured foreign investor.[136] However, pursuing the host state's illegal act by the investor might be pointless as there is a big likelihood that the judges might be unfair, politically biased and/or discriminatory. Thus, the process in the host state might have an unfair outcome.

6.3.4. Remedies provided by investor-state-contracts

It is possible that a state may agree in addition to an existing BIT or MIT to protect the investor's rights on the basis of a contract, in which also possible remedies are awarded to an injured investor for the wrongful actions or omissions, and the legal consequences which flow therefrom by the host state.[137] Such remedies can be found in the contract which generally regulates the specific investment (e.g., an investor acquires shares in a state-owned company and commits to make additional investments by providing a certain amount of capital and to pursue certain business activities). The major difference between these kinds of contracts and any other commercial contract between two legal entities is that one of the parties is a state, while the other is a business entity.

---

a violation of the BIT. An example of an umbrella clause is Article X of the Switzerland-Philippines BIT, which provides that *"[e]ach Contracting Party shall observe any obligation it has assumed with regard to specific investments in its territory by investors of the other Contracting Party."* Cf. JARROD WONG, Umbrella clauses in bilateral investment treaties: Of breaches of contract, treaty violations, and the divide between developing and developed countries in foreign investment disputes, 14 Geo. Mason L. Rev. 137 (2006), p. 144.

[136] Cf. JARROD HEPBURN, Domestic law in international investment arbitration (2017), pp. 73 et seq.

[137] JOSÉ ENRIQUE ALVAREZ, The public international law regime governing international investment (2011), p. 129.

IV. Nationalization

1. Generally

Nationalization is the process of taking private property from an owner into public ownership by a state through a wide range of governmental acts.[138] Nationalization may happen not just in developing countries, but also in developed countries (notably during an economic crisis, as evidenced during the latest crisis in this century). However, nationalization is sometimes indispensable as means to achieve some legitimate public interest of a state (e.g., a state nationalizes private property in order to build a road or other infrastructure projects). The international law of nationalization has been the subject of various conflicts.

The customary international law on nationalization has been developed during the time of confiscations with regard to cross-border investment projects.[139] It is noteworthy that following the period of decolonization, revolutions and spreading communism there was an intense period in the 50s and 60s of the last century, when numerous nationalizations and seizures of foreign property happened and the states argued over the lawfulness of these acts and the compensation. Moreover, due to the shortage of oil in the 1970s there have been various oil nationalizations of oil supplies in this decade (e.g., Iraq: 1972; India: 1973 coal industry and oil companies). Furthermore, there were in the last years some cases of expropriations in relation with foreign investments in the energy sector.[140] In Spring 2023 a

---

[138] Definition found on: https://www.merriam-webster.com/dictionary/nationalization. The opposite of nationalization is usually privatization or de-nationalization.

[139] Cf. also ANDREW NEWCOMBE/LUÍS PARADELL, Law and practice of investment treaties, standards of treatment (2009), p. 322 and American International Group, Inc./American Life Insurance Company and Islamic Republic of Iran/Central Insurance of Iran (Bimeh Markazi Iran), Case No. 2, Award No. 93-2-3.

[140] E.g., nationalization of banks in Greece, Iceland, the Netherlands, Portugal, but there are also examples of nationalization of other industries, notably those of general economic interest (e.g., recently, in Japan and United Kingdom). Cf. also BREAU, op. cit., pp. 155 et seq. and JOHN WILLMAN, Nationalisation: a blast from the past, in:

nationalization has been discussed in Switzerland with regard to the Credit Suisse fiasco.

Types of nationalizations in the broader sense in the field of cross border investment projects[141]

(i)   Expropriation

Expropriation is when a state takes over a foreign investment in a country by the state or a state-mandated third party.

(ii)   Nationalization

Nationalization is when a state takes over a whole sector of economy with its foreign investments in a country by the state or a state-mandated third party.

(iii)   Confiscation

Confiscation is an unlawful takeover of a foreign investment by the state or a state-mandated third party.

Furthermore, it is possible to subdivide expropriation, nationalization and confiscation into:

(i)   Direct expropriation/nationalization/confiscation

A direct expropriation/nationalization/confiscation happens if a state passes or applies a specific legislation to takeover another's property.

(ii)   Indirect expropriation/nationalization/confiscation

An indirect expropriation/nationalization/confiscation happens when the foreign investor is losing the control or economic value of his investment project through the interference by the host state, even when the legal title of the investment is not affected.

Financial Times (January 18, 2018).
[141] Cf. ROGER E. MEINERS/AL. H. RINGLEB/FRANCES L. EDWARDS, The legal environment of business (2018), p. 549 and NEWCOMBE/PARADELL, op. cit., pp. 324 et seq.

(iii) Creeping expropriation/nationalization/confiscation
Creeping expropriation/nationalization/confiscation happens incrementally or step by step through a series of separate governmental measures or acts, none of which might qualify as an expropriation/ nationalization/confiscation by itself, but altogether they have the effect to destroy the value of the investment and lead also to a de facto dispossession.

2. Legality of nationalization

2.1. General rule

Most of the tribunals, state practice and international instruments are of the opinion that a state can nationalize private property or even a sector whenever it wants. The base of this rule is the territorial sovereignty of a state and the legality of the act is founded on the willingness to pay a compensation.

A state may nationalize the property of foreign investors within its borders in a lawful way, if
(1) the nationalization is based on a public interest/purpose;
(2) it has been taken following proper law proceedings;
(3) it is non-discriminatory; and
(4) a compensation will be paid.

2.1.1. Case law

Ethyl Corporation v. the Government of Canada
Award on jurisdiction in the NAFTA/UNCITRAL case between Ethyl Corporation and the Government of Canada, June 24, 1998
In April 1997 the Government of Canada passed a law restricting the import and interprovincial transport of the neuro-toxic MMT, a gasoline additive that contains the heavy metal manganese.

On April 15, 1997, Ethyl Corporation, an American legal entity with a Canadian subsidiary, invoked the *"expropriation-clause"* (article 1110) of the investment chapter of NAFTA to sue the Government of Canada for CAD 350 million for damages and lost income, because the law was a measure tantamount to an expropriation.

On July 20, 1998, the Government of Canada decided to settle the dispute. It issued a statement that the manganese-based additive is neither a health nor an environmental risk and paid a compensation of CAD 19.5 million to the Ethyl Corporation.

Methanex Corporation v. United States of America

Decision on amici curiae: Methanex Corporation v United States, Ad hoc—UNCITRAL Arbitration Rules; IIC 165 (2001), January 15, 2001

Partial award: Methanex Corporation v. United States, Ad hoc—UNCITRAL Arbitration Rules; IIC 166 (2002), August 7, 2002

Methanex, a Canadian company, is a major producer of methanol, a key component in MTBE (methyl tertiary butyl ether), which is used to increase the oxygen content and can act as an octane enhancer for unleaded gasoline.

The Californian government enacted a law banning the use of MTBE in reformulated gasoline in California, because it was of the opinion that the additive is contaminating drinking water supplies, and is therefore posing a significant risk to human health, safety, and the environment.

In response, Methanex and its American subsidiaries launched an international arbitration against the United States. The company argued that the law is ineffective and non-enforcement of domestic environmental laws is responsible for the presence of MTBE in California water supplies. Furthermore, it invoked the *"expropriation-clause"* (article 1110) of the investment chapter of NAFTA and argued that the planned ban is tantamount to an expropriation of the company's investment as it was not anymore allowed to sell these products. Thus, the legal entity was seeking financial compensation from the United States in the amount of over USD 900 million.

On August 9, 2005, the tribunal released the final award, dismissing all of the claims. The Tribunal ordered Methanex to pay the United States' legal fees and arbitral expenses in the amount of approximately USD 4 million.

The tribunal undertook an extensive review of the process by which California enacted its ban and held in a final award that (Final Award, Part IV, Chapter D, para 7 and 15): *"In the Tribunal's view, Methanex is correct that an intentionally discriminatory regulation against a foreign investor fulfils a key requirement for establishing expropriation. But as a matter of general international law, a non-discriminatory regulation for a public purpose, which is enacted in accordance with due process and, which affects, inter alias, a foreign investor or investment is not deemed expropriatory and compensable unless specific commitments had been given by the regulating government to the then putative foreign investor contemplating investment that the government would refrain from such regulation ... For reasons elaborated here and earlier in this Award, the Tribunal concludes that the California ban was made for a public purpose, was non-discriminatory and was accomplished with due process. Hence, Methanex's central claim under Article 1110(1) of expropriation under one of the three forms of action in that provision fails. From the standpoint of international law, the California ban was a lawful regulation and not an expropriation."*

Ronald S. Lauder v. the Czech Republic

Final award UNCITRAL arbitration, September 3, 2001

In the final award it was held that: *"The Bilateral Investment Treaties generally do not define the term of expropriation and nationalization, or any of the other terms denoting similar measures of forced dispossession ("dispossession", "taking", "deprivation", or "privation"). Furthermore, the practice shows that although the various terms may be used either alone or in combination, most often no distinctions have been attempted between the general concept of dispossession and the specific forms thereof. In general, expropriation means the coercive appropriation by the state of private property, usually by means of individual administrative measures.*

Nationalization involves large-scale takings on the basis of an executive or legislative act for the purpose of transferring property or interests into the public domain. The concept of indirect (or "de facto", or "creeping") expropriation is not clearly defined. Indirect expropriation or nationalization is a measure that does not involve an overt taking, but that effectively neutralizes the enjoyment of the property. It is generally accepted that a wide variety of measures are susceptible to lead to indirect expropriation, and each case is therefore to be decided on the basis of its attending circumstances (Rudolf Dolzer & Margrete Stevens, Bilateral Investment Treaties, p. 98-100 (1995); Georgio Sacerdoti, Bilateral Treaties and Multilateral Instruments on Investment Protection, 379-382 (1997)). The European Court of Human Rights in Mellacher and Others v. Austria (1989 Eur.Ct.H.R. (ser. A, No. 169)), held that a "formal" expropriation is a measure aimed at a "transfer of property", while a "de facto" expropriation occurs when a state deprives the owner of his "right to use, let or sell (his) property"."

2.1.2. State practice

Hull principle[142]

United States State Department Letter to the Mexican Government (1938)

In 1938 the United States Secretary of State Cordell Hull held in a letter to the Mexican government regarding the nationalization of certain agrarian and oil properties, that expropriation of foreign owned property is legitimate but it must be accompanied by *"prompt, adequate, and effective compensation"*. According to this view, the nationalizing state is obligated under international law to pay the deprived party the full value of the property taken.

---

[142] FRANK G. DAWSON/BURNS H. WESTON, "Prompt, adequate and effective": a universal standard of compensation?, in: 30 Fordham L. Rev. (1962), pp. 733-734; DAVID COLLINS, An introduction of international investment law (2017), p. 188 and SORNARAJAH, International law, p. 210.

2.1.3. International instruments

1962 General Assembly Resolution 1803 (XVII): The declaration on permanent sovereignty over natural resources

In 1962, the United Nations General Assembly adopted Resolution 1803, *"Permanent Sovereignty over National Resources"*, which states in article 4 that in the event of nationalization, the owner *"shall be paid appropriate compensation in accordance with international law."*

Energy Charter Treaty

The Energy Charter Treaty (ECT) is an international agreement, which establishes a multilateral framework for cross border co-operations in the energy industry. The treaty covers all aspects of commercial energy activities including trade, transit, investments and energy efficiency. The treaty is legally binding and includes dispute resolution procedures.

Article 13 of the ECT provides a guarantee that both direct and indirect forms of expropriation of an investment shall only take place against prompt effective and adequate compensation, by following due process and on a non-discriminatory basis. This is similar to the guarantee found in most of the BITs, including those signed by ECT member countries.

Article 13(1) states the following: *"Investments of Investors of a Contracting Party in the Area of any other Contracting Party shall not be nationalized, expropriated or subjected to a measure or measures having effect equivalent to nationalization or expropriation (hereinafter referred to as "Expropriation") except where such Expropriation is:*

(a) for a purpose which is in the public interest;
(b) not discriminatory;
(c) carried out under due process of law; and
(d) accompanied by the payment of prompt, adequate and effective compensation."

2.2. Public interest/purpose of the nationalization

Different countries have different views about what is a public interest or public purpose, which justifies a nationalization. *"Public Purpose"* has been defined as *"reasons of public utility, judicial liquidation and similar measures"* (CHORZÓW FACTORY). Thus, challenging a nationalization based on a claim that was not in the *"public interest"* would possibly be effective in the case of a dictator seizing property clearly for his personal use.[143] In any event, public purpose or public interest is a legal standard which is generally not defined by legislation *in abstracto*, but it is rather imperative to take into account all the circumstances of the individual case.

> **Siderman de Blake v. Republic of Argentina**
>
> (Siderman de Blake v. Republic of Argentina, 965 F.2d. 699 [9th Cir.] 1992)
>
> The night before the overthrow of the Argentine government by the military in 1976, an Argentine citizen was tortured, and he, his wife, and his son were expelled from Argentina. In addition, Argentina expropriated an Argentine corporation owned by the family through a sham *"judicial intervention"* in 1977. Included among the property of this corporation was the hotel *"Gran Corona"*, in Tucumán, Argentina.
>
> The Sidermans' brought suit it the United States District Court, but the court dismissed the expropriation claims. The Sidermans' appealed to the Ninth Circuit Court of Appeals, which held that the actions of the Argentine government fell within the *"commercial activities"* exception of the US Foreign Sovereign Immunities Act (FISA), and remanded the case to the district court. In particular, the court held that the Sidermans' claim was *"based upon a commercial activity carried on in the United States by the foreign state."* First, Argentina's continuous management and operation of the hotel, and receipt of profits from the hotel, were commercial activities in which a private party might engage. Second, these activities were being carried on in the

---

[143] Cf. NEWCOMBE/PARADELL, op. cit., p. 371.

United States, due to the advertising of the hotel in the United States and the solicitation of American guests through the national airline of Argentina, which was its agent. The hotel also accepted American credit cards.

Thus, the Argentine government expropriated a hotel in which a citizen of the United States of America held an interest. Furthermore, the court held that actions by the Argentinian government violated international law:

(i) *Public Purpose of Expropriation*: The hotel was taken for the profit of the government, and not for any public purpose.

(ii) *Expropriation was discriminatory*: Since it was based on the fact that the Sidermans' were Jews; Christians were not expropriated.

(iii) *Compensation*: No compensation for the expropriated hotel was paid.

Based on this, the court held that the expropriation was illegal under international law, and the sovereign immunity defense was not effective.

2.3. Property has been taken following proper law proceedings

The domestic law of the host state has to be enacted following the proper law proceedings, and to precise the process for carrying out a nationalization of the investor's properties. There has to be *"an actual and substantive legal procedure for a foreign investor to raise its claims against the depriving actions already taken or about to be taken against it. Some basic legal mechanisms, such as reasonable advance notice, a fair hearing and an unbiased and impartial adjudicator to assess the actions in dispute, are expected to be readily available and accessible to the investor to make such legal procedure meaningful."*[144]

---

[144] Cf. ADC Affiliate Limited and ADC & ADMC Management Limited v. Republic of Hungary, ICSID Case No. ARB/03/16, Serial No. 120, para. 434 et seq.; C. L. LIM/JEAN HO/MARTINS PAPARINSKIS, International investment law and arbitration, (2018), pp. 343-344 and KRISTA NADAKAVUKAREN SCHEFER, International investment

Proper law proceedings comprise any issue in connection with the process which determines an objective evaluation of the process, such as what should be taken into account, limitations to discretionary powers, which state body of law has to make a decision, time limit for the decision, appropriate recourse before the court of law etc. Since courts are often also involved in the process (and preferably a court makes the decision and not a government's ministry, agency or other office of the executive branch), the appropriateness of the whole process is intrinsically linked with the general position of the judiciary and its independence, fairness, objectivity and impartiality.

2.4. Non-discrimination

An expropriation must also be *"non-discriminatory"* to be considered *"legal"* under international law.

> **Oscar Chinn**
> PCIJ Series A/B No. 63 (1934)
> The Permanent Court of International Justice defined discrimination as follows (para. 93): *"The form of discrimination which is forbidden is therefore discrimination based upon nationality and involving differential treatment by reason of their nationality as between persons belonging to different national groups."*

A discriminatory taking is a taking that unreasonably singles out a particular person or group of people, i.e., when a specific nationality is targeted.[145] Thus, in 1959 the Indonesian nationalizations of Dutch property were clearly violations of the international law.[146] Broadly speaking, most often discrimination in nationalization cases is based on nationality. However, discrimination are also possible based

---

law, text, cases and materials (2016), pp. 204-205.
[145] Cf. also the aforementioned case SIDERMAN DE BLAKE V. REPUBLIC OF ARGENTINA.
[146] Cf. also DAMOS DUMOI AGUSMAN, Treaties under Indonesian law: A comparative study (2014), p. 8 and LOWENFELD, op. cit., p. 522.

on other grounds (gender, religion, age, place of residence, financial census etc.).

2.5. Compensation

2.5.1 Generally

It is the generally accepted view in the field of public international law, that a nationalization requires the payment of a compensation. Already in older cases the tribunals stated this rule (cf. for example CHORZÓW FACTORY). Also, in modern tribunal decisions like in the ETHYL CORPORATION V. THE GOVERNMENT OF CANADA or newer ICSID-decisions it is held that a compensation must be paid.

However, if the nationalization is considered illegal, then the host state has usually to restitute in kind and if this is not possible, it has very often to pay damages, which go beyond a compensation as they include a *"punishment"*.

> **Chorzów Factory**
>
> Factory at Chorzow (Germ. v. Pol.), Series A.-No. 17, September 13, 1928, Collection of Judgments, No. 13, Case concerning the factory at Chorzów, para. 125:
>
> *"The essential principle contained in the actual notion of an illegal act – a principle which seems to be established by international practice and in particular by the decisions of arbitral tribunals – is that reparation must, as far as possible, wipe-out all the consequences of the illegal act and re-establish the situation which would, in all probability, have existed if that act had not been committed. Restitution in kind, or, if this is not possible, payment of a sum corresponding to the value which a restitution in kind would bear; the award, if need be, of damages for loss sustained which would not be covered by restitution in kind or payment in place of it. Such are the principles which should serve to determine the amount of compensation due for an act contrary to international law."*

2.5.2. Full compensation v. appropriate compensation

Although there is the common opinion that in the event of a nationalization a compensation has to be paid, there are different views whether the compensation has to be full or appropriate.

(i) Full compensation

In order to indemnify a foreign investor fully, the compensation has to encompass the value of structures, machines, business, goodwill and future profits. Even though this standard of compensation is supported by the majority of capital-exporting states, customary practice is in this regard not uniform. Most states have subscribed to the standard of full compensation in BITs, though in some MITs the same states have promoted different standards.[147] As mentioned before, UNITED STATES SECRETARY OF STATE CORDELL HULL held in his letter to the Mexican Government that the consideration has to be "*full (adequate), prompt, effective.*" This state practice has for example also been restated in article 13(1) ECT and means the following:

(i.1) Full/Adequate

The criteria "*adequate*" refers to the question of the amount. Eventually, a foreign investor has to be in the same position as if his property has not been nationalized. This means that he has to receive the market value of its investment project (assets etc.) including future profits.[148]

---

[147] Cf. SORNARAJAH, International law, p. 417 and 437 and GUIGUO WANG, International investment law: a Chinese perspective (2015), p. 450.

[148] Cf. SERGEY RIPINSKY/KEVIN WILLIAMS, Damages in international investment law (2008), p. 71 and SANGWANI PATRICK NG'AMBI, Resource nationalism in international investment law (2016), pp. 78-79. Market value is the price an asset will get in the market place.

(i.2)   Prompt

The payment of the compensation has to be paid quickly after the nationalization. There should not be any unreasonable delay (e.g., the compensation will be paid from the future profits of the nationalized legal entity).[149]

(i.3)   Effective

The currency, in which the compensation will be paid, should be freely convertible; a payment in local currency is not considered as effective.[150]

(ii)   Appropriate compensation

However, there is also the view that the amount of the compensation has to be decided on a case-by-case basis and therefore the compensation has to be *"appropriate"* (e.g., article 4 of the General Assembly Resolution 1803 [XVII]: The declaration on permanent sovereignty over natural resources).[151] This means in order to determine the compensation a tribunal has to look at the excessive profits, investments, ability of host state to pay the indemnification, the caused environmental damage etc.[152]

This standard represents more the position of developing countries as the *"appropriate compensation"*-standard allows them to pay less than full compensation following a nationalization. This idea was also supported by the so-called *"Calvo Doctrine"*, which requires that the

---

[149] Cf. DAVID COLLINS, An introduction to international investment law (2017), p. 188 and JUNJI NAKAGAWA, Nationalization, natural resources and international investment law, contractual relationship as a dynamic bargaining process (2018), p. 128.

[150] Cf. ALAN W. FORD, The Anglo-Iranian oil dispute of 1951-1952: a study of the role of law in the relations of states (1954), p. 324 and E. I. NWOGUGU, The legal problems of foreign investment in developing countries (1965), p. 56.

[151] Cf. NG'AMBI, op. cit., pp. 80-81.

[152] Cf. ADAMU KYUKA USMAN, Theory and practice of international economic law (2017), p. 216. The net book value is the value of an asset in the books of a legal entity.

compensation should be determined by local law, because it is a question of sovereignty.[153]

(iii) Application by tribunals and courts

National courts as well as tribunals applied public international law on the question of the legality of a nationalization and compensation. In these judicial precedents, which are according to article 38 of the ICJ-Statute a source of international law, it has been held that nationalizations are legal as long as all the aforementioned conditions are respected. However, with regard to the standard of the compensation, it is not clear to which of the two approaches the judges tend to follow.

There are various tribunal decisions (e.g., CHORZÓW FACTORY or BARCELONA TRACTION), which favor the *"full compensation-standard"*. However, there have been contrary views like in the below mentioned AMINOIL-CASE, where it was considered on the question of compensation, that it is possible to advocate an *"appropriate compensation"*.

Aminoil

Award in the matter of an arbitration between Kuwait and the American Independent Oil Company (AMINOIL)

Vol. 21, No. 5 (September 1982), pp. 976-1053

In 1948 a so-called *"colonial-concession"* for 60 years was given by the United Kingdom to the American Independent Oil Company (AMINOIL) in order to exploit oil in Kuwait. Before the 60 years period was over, the government of Kuwait revoked the agreement in passing a law (decree) and took over the operation. AMINOIL alleged that this was illegal, and wanted to characterize this as an international dispute in order to get out of domestic courts. However, the

---

[153] OECD, International investment law, a changing landscape, a companion volume to international investment perspectives (2005), p. 44 and DAVID COLLINS, The BRIC states and outward foreign direct investment (2013), p. 205.

validity of this decree had to be argued, because AMINOIL alleged that the nationalization was discriminatory.

1) Discriminatory nationalization

AMINOIL said that they were discriminated because the nationalization just touched an American company; nothing has been done to the Arabian Oil Company, which was in the similar situation. Therefore, not the totality of the sector was affected, and thus it is not a nationalization. The Court held that the operations of the aforementioned companies were under objective criteria different. There have been adequate reasons for not nationalizing the Arabian Oil Company, because it had a much more complex production (high-cost off-shore production, which required a high degree of expertise, and therefore it was not that easy to take-over), and also the concession was different. Furthermore, there was nothing in the law, which showed that the government of Kuwait was only after American companies. Kuwait had nationalized over 90 % of the petroleum production in its territory.

2) Infringement of stabilization clauses

In the Concession Agreement of 1948 were the following provisions: Article 1: *"The period of this Agreement shall be sixty (60) years from the date of signature."*; Article 17: *"The Sheikh shall not by general or by administrative measures or by any other act whatever annul this Agreement ... No alteration shall be made in the terms of this Agreement by either the Sheikh or the Company except in the event of the Sheikh and the Company jointly agreeing that it is desirable in the interest of both parties to make certain alterations, deletions or additions to this agreement."* In 1961 a new Article 11 was provided for the Concession Agreement of 1948: *"... this Agreement shall not be terminated before the expiration of the period specified in Article 1 ..."*.

With regard to these provisions AMINOIL maintained the view that these clauses constituted so-called *"stabilization-clauses"* of the contract, and a straightforward and direct reading of them lead to the conclusion that they prohibit any nationalization. The Government of Kuwait argued that, on the contrary, these clauses did not prevent a nationalization, because:

1. the provisions of the Kuwait Constitution prevent the state from granting stabilization guarantees by contract; and
2. permanent sovereignty over natural resources has become an imperative rule of *jus cogens* prohibiting states from affording, by contract or by treaty, guarantees of any kind against the exercise of the public authority in regard to all matters relating to natural riches.

The Court held that it did not appear from the constitutional provisions that they prevented in any way the state from granting stabilization guarantees by contract. Furthermore, domestic law cannot be used as e defense for violating international law, especially if the state has deliberately agreed to enter into a contract/treaty. And with regard to the last argument that even if United Nations General Assembly Resolution 1803 (XVII) adopted in 1962, is to be regarded as reflecting the state of international law, such is not the case with subsequent resolutions which have not the same degree of authority. Even if some of their provisions can be regarded as codifying rules that reflect international practice, it would not be possible from this to deduce the existence of a rule of international law prohibiting a state from undertaking not to proceed to nationalization during a limited period of time. No rule from public international law prevents a state from nationalizing. Moreover, the *"stabilization"* clauses do not prevent a state from nationalizations. However, clauses like the ones *in casu* create legitimate expectations of AMINOIL that they can invest and subsequently make business in Kuwait for a period of 60 years.

3) Standard of compensation

The tribunal rejected that the compensation has to be made on the book value of the nationalized foreign investment, because in this situation it is not appropriate. It took a case-by-case approach in order to see what is appropriate and held the following: *"The Tribunal considers that the determination of the amount of an award of "appropriate" compensation is better carried out by means of an enquiry into all the circumstances relevant to the particular concrete case..."* Furthermore, the *legitimate expectation* has to be compensated. AMINOIL had because of the *"stabilization"*-clause a legitimate expectation in a *"reasonable rate of return"*. The tribunal looked at the case, the history, the behavior of AMINOIL and referred to the *"appropriate compensation"* as the applicable standard as it cited Article 4 of United Nations General Assembly Resolution 1803 (XVII) of December 14, 1962 instead of a full compensation.

V. Investment insurance

1. Generally

Companies do not only assess the possible profitability of their endeavors, but they are also concerned with the risks linked to their investments in the host state. Especially, cross-border transactions and investments are exposed to more risks than domestic transactions and investments, as they face not only commercial risks but also non-commercial risks. These non-commercial risks include currency issues, restriction of transfer of funds, revenues and/or profits, governmental expropriation or confiscation, civil disturbance, insurrection, civil strife, revolution, war or breach of contract. Particularly with regard to developing countries, these risks affect investments negatively as investors generally want to invest in states that have no or low non-commercial risks.[154]

However, the aforementioned non-commercial risks can be mitigated by means of appropriately structured insurances. These insurances are designed to protect a company against the losses occurring due to specific risks.[155] There are not just private insurance companies, which offer these products, but also international and national financial institutions that provide political risk insurances. These schemes have a positive influence on international business and the investment climate, and many of these insurances have a substantial coverage.[156]

---

[154] Cf. SALACUSE, The three laws of international investment, p. 258; THOMAS E. KRAYENBUEHL, Cross-border exposures and country risk: Assessment and Monitoring (2001), pp. 42 et seq. and 114-115. and R. BARRY JOHNSTON/İNCI ÖTKER-ROBE, A modernized approach to managing the risks in cross-border capital movements, IMF Policy Working Paper No. 99/6 (1999), p. 8.

[155] VERNON K. JACOBS/N. RICHARD FOX, Risk management for amateur investors, A guide to higher yields with less risk for nonprofessional investors, plus an analysis of the impact of the new tax law on investors (2003), pp. 10-11.

[156] Cf. WARRICK SMITH, Covering political and regulatory risks: Issues and options for private infrastructure arrangements, in: Dealing with public risk in private infrastructure, edited by Timothy Irwin/Michael Klein/Guillermo E. Perry/Mateen Thobani (1997),

A company has the following possibilities to insure a cross border investment project.

1.1. State insurance schemes

Many capital-exporting states operate their own agencies issuing non-commercial risk insurance (e.g., Japan: EID/MITI, United States: U.S. International Development Finance Corporation [DFC], Germany: TREUARBEIT, United Kingdom: United Kingdom Export Finance [UKEF], France: Compagnie Française d'Assurance pour le Commerce Extérieur [Coface]). These agencies offer insurance programs, which are in competition with the ones offered by a private insurer.[157] For example, it is somehow more advantageous for an investor from the United States to obtain an insurance from DFC, because there has to be a BIT between the United States and the host state and after subrogation of the insured claim, the United States will usually not have the same problem with recovery and enforcement as the investor would have.

1.2. Multilateral international insurance scheme

The Multilateral Investment Guarantee Agency (MIGA) was established in 1988 by an international treaty, operates out of Washington, D.C., United States, and is an enormous organization with 182 member governments (154 developing and 28 industrialized countries). The World Bank supports it. MIGA is the most known international insurance scheme.[158]

---

p. 68 and SCOTT L. HOFFMANN, The law and business of international project finance: a resource for governments, sponsors, lenders, lawyers, and project participants (2001), p. 411.

[157] PRISCILLA A. AHMED/XINGHAI FANG, Project finance in developing countries: IFC's lessons of experience (1999), p. 36.

[158] Cf. https://www.miga.org/history.

1.3. Private insurance schemes

As mentioned, there are also private insurances, which are insuring investment projects in foreign developing countries. However, these insurances are often limited and more expensive than the governmental schemes.[159]

1.4. Combination of these types of insurances

It is possible to combine several of the above-mentioned insurance schemes (e.g., it is possible that a legal entity covers 50% of the non-commercial risks by MIGA and the other 50% by DFC). Sometimes state insurance schemes work together with MIGA for insuring big projects, and thus are creating a consortium in order to guarantee an insurance coverage for these investments.[160]

2. MIGA (Multilateral Investment Guarantee Agency)

2.1. Generally

MIGA (Multilateral Investment Guarantee Agency) was established in 1988 by an international treaty, is headquartered in Washington D.C., USA, and supported by the World Bank. It was created to promote foreign direct investment into developing countries. The organization was founded with a capital base of USD 1 billion.

Unlike other insurers, MIGA is backed by the World Bank Group and its member countries. According to article 1(b) of the MIGA-Convention MIGA has *"juridical personality"*, and has the right to *"institute legal proceedings"*. MIGA also requires host country government approval for every project. Thus, it tries to work with host governments and to resolve claims before they are filed.

---

[159] AHMED/FANG, op. cit., p. 36.
[160] Cf. as an example: Albania, Business and investment opportunities yearbook, Volume 1, Strategic, practical information and opportunities, (2016), p. 220.

MIGA has paid several claims since 1988. The first claim was in 2000 for an equity investment by P.T. East Java Power Corporation in Indonesia. The project was one of several power projects suspended by a presidential decree in 1997 in response to the country's economic crisis in the late 1990s. The second claim was for war and civil disturbance relating to a power plant project in Nepal. MIGA paid compensation for the repair of the damages of the gas turbine, and the project continues to be in operation. The third claim was for a project in Argentina at the time of the country's financial crisis. The fourth and fifth claim were paid in 2009 and were both related to losses under war and civil disturbance coverage. One was paid for losses incurred in the violence following Kenya's disputed election in 2007 and the other was paid for losses resulting from political violence in Madagascar. In 2011, a small claim for war and civil disturbance was paid from the donor-funded Afghanistan Investment Guarantee Facility. In 2015 MIGA paid three claims for losses incurred from war and civil disturbance events, in Burkina Faso, Central African Republic, and Mali.

The small number of claims paid by MIGA since 1988 attests to the agency's ability to work with investors and host countries to find amicable resolutions to disputes. MIGA focuses on finding solutions to pre-claim situations before they reach the level of full-fledged claims. MIGA's proactive facilitation efforts have been important in the resolution of more than 90 disputes related to MIGA-guaranteed projects.

2.2. Purpose

MIGA's stated mission is *"to promote foreign direct investment into developing countries to support economic growth, reduce poverty, and improve people's lives"*. Therefore, it is written in article 2 of the MIGA-Convention that MIGA's principal purpose and objective is to encourage the flow of investment to and among member countries by means of guarantees. MIGA provides guarantees against non-commercial risks to protect cross border investments in member countries. Guarantees protect investors against the risks of currency transfer restriction, expropriation, war, terrorism and civil disturbance, and breach of contract.

MIGA is based on a multilateral treaty and therefore interesting for countries without national insurance schemes. Furthermore, if for example the United States do not have a BIT with a specific country, then DFC cannot apply. However, there is still the possibility of obtaining an insurance from MIGA.

2.3. Eligible insureds[161]

In general, investors who are citizens of, or entities that are incorporated in MIGA member countries – other than the host country, in which the investment is being made – are eligible for MIGA guarantees. However, MIGA can insure an investment made by a national of a host country if the funds to be invested come from outside the country and the application for coverage is made jointly by the investor and the host country.

As nearly every state is member of MIGA, it is possible to get virtually for every country on earth a MIGA-insurance.

2.4. Eligible host countries

Article 14 MIGA-Convention states that *"[i]nvestments shall be guaranteed ... if they are to be made in the territory of a developing member country"*. In order to determine which states are considered to be a developing country, MIGA consults the World Bank's classification list. Additionally, there must be a good investment climate.

2.5. Insured investments[162]

MIGA insures cross border investments. This includes projects with new investments as well as investments

---

[161] Cf. http://www.miga.org/sites/default/files/archive/Documents/miga_documents/IGGen_old.pdf.
[162] Cf. http://www.miga.org/sites/default/files/archive/Documents/

associated with the expansion, modernization, improvement, or enhancement of existing projects, or where the investor demonstrates both the development benefits of and a long-term commitment to the project. Acquisitions by new investors, including the privatization of state-owned enterprises, may also be eligible.

Forms of eligible investments include equity interests, shareholder and non-shareholder loans, loan guarantees, as well as certain types of transactions in which the remuneration of the investor largely depends on the revenues or production of the investment project (e.g., technical assistance contracts, management contracts, operating leases, profit sharing contracts, and franchising agreements).

MIGA will not insure unless the investment:

(1) is financially viable,
(2) contributes to the host country,
(3) is consistent with the host country's developing goals,
(4) complies with MIGA's Policy on Social and Environmental Sustainability and Anti-corruption and Fraud Standards, and
(5) has appropriate legal protection for investors in the host country.

Before MIGA insures, it has to evaluate the investment project and thus it will:

(1) do a project assessment,
(2) do a risk assessment,
(3) obtain a host country approval (article 15 MIGA-Convention).

Most sectors are eligible for MIGA guarantees, including (but not limited to) financial, infrastructure, oil and gas and mining projects, telecommunications, services, agribusiness, and manufacturing. Sectors not eligible for coverage include gambling, tobacco production and processing, highly speculative investments, defense, illegal drugs, and the production of spirits.

---

miga_documents/IGGen_old.pdf.

2.6. Insurable risks[163]

2.6.1. Generally

The insurance guarantees protect investors against the risks of currency inconvertibility and transfer restriction, expropriation, breach of contract (for contracts between the investor/project enterprise and the authorities of the host country), and war, terrorism and civil disturbance. These coverages may be purchased individually or in combination.

2.6.2. Currency inconvertibility and transfer restriction[164]

The insurance for currency inconvertibility and transfer restriction protects against losses arising from an investor's inability to legally convert local currency (capital, interest, principal, profits, royalties, and other remittances) into foreign exchange and/or to transfer local currency or foreign exchange outside the country where such a situation results from a government action or failure to act. Currency depreciation is not covered. In the event of a claim, MIGA pays compensation in the currency specified in the contract of guarantee.

2.6.3. Expropriation[165]

The insurance guarantee for expropriation prevents losses arising from certain government actions that may reduce or eliminate ownership of, control over, or rights to the insured investment. In addition to outright nationalization and confiscation, *"creeping"* expropriation – a series of acts that, over time, have an expropriatory effect – is also covered. Coverage is available on a limited basis for partial expropriation (e.g., confiscation of funds or tangible assets).

In the case of total expropriation of equity investments, compensation to the insured party is based on the net book

---

[163] Cf. https://www.miga.org/products.
[164] Cf. https://www.miga.org/product/currency-inconvertibility-and-transfer-restriction.
[165] Cf. https://www.miga.org/product/expropriation.

value of the insured investment. For expropriation of funds, MIGA pays the insured portion of the blocked funds. For loans and loan guaranties, MIGA can insure the outstanding principal and any accrued and unpaid interest. Compensation will be paid upon assignment of the investor's interest in the expropriated investment (e.g., equity shares or interest in a loan agreement) to MIGA.

2.6.4. Breach of contract[166]

The insurance for breach of contract protects against losses arising from the government's breach or repudiation of a contract with the investor. Breach of contract coverage may be extended to the contractual obligations of state-owned enterprises in certain circumstances. In the event of an alleged breach or repudiation, the investor should invoke a dispute resolution mechanism (e.g., an arbitration) set out in the underlying contract. If, after a specified period of time, the investor has been unable to obtain an award due to the government's frustration of its efforts, or has obtained an award but the investor has not received payment under the award, MIGA will pay compensation. If certain conditions are met, MIGA may, at its discretion, make a provisional payment pending the outcome of the dispute. MIGA may also elect to pay compensation without an award, if the investor does not have recourse to a dispute resolution forum or there is unreasonable government interference with the investor's pursuit of legal rights against the host government. The coverages described above may be purchased individually or in combination, but selection of the desired coverages must be made by an investor before MIGA issues its guarantee.

2.6.5. War, terrorism and civil disturbance[167]

The insurance guarantee for war, terrorism and civil disturbance protects against loss from, damage to, or the

---

[166] Cf. https://www.miga.org/product/breach-contract.
[167] https://www.miga.org/product/war-terrorism-and-civil-disturbance.

destruction or disappearance of, tangible assets or total business interruption (the total inability to conduct operations essential to a project's overall financial viability) caused by politically motivated acts of war or civil disturbance in the country, including revolution, insurrection, coups d'état, sabotage, and terrorism. The cover protects against losses directly attributable to the physical damage of assets and total business interruption. For total business interruption, compensation would be based on the net book value of the total insured equity investment or the insured portion of the principal and interest payment in default as a direct result of a covered war and civil disturbance event. For tangible asset losses, MIGA will pay the investor's share of the lesser of the book value of the project assets, their replacement cost, and the cost of repair of the damaged assets.

Temporary business interruption may also be included upon a request from the investor and would cover three sources of interruption: (i) damage of assets, (ii) forced abandonment, and (iii) loss of use. For short-term business interruption, MIGA will pay unavoidable continuing expenses and extraordinary expenses associated with the restart of operations and lost business income or, in the case of loans, missed payments.

This coverage encompasses not only violence in the host country directed against a host country government, but also against foreign governments or foreign investments, including the investor's government or nationality.

2.6.6. Non-honoring of financial obligations[168]

The non-honoring of financial obligations coverage provides protection against losses resulting from a failure of a sovereign, sub-sovereign, or state-owned enterprise to make a payment when due under an unconditional financial payment obligation or guarantee related to an eligible investment. It does not require the investor to obtain an arbitral award. This coverage is applicable in situations when a financial payment obligation is unconditional and

---

[168] https://www.miga.org/product/non-honoring-financial-obligations.

not subject to defenses. Compensation is based on the insured outstanding principal and any accrued and unpaid interest.

2.7. Duration[169]

MIGA issues guarantees for periods for more than 1 year and a maximum of up to 15 years, and occasionally, 20 years if it is justified by the nature of the project. In guarantees that cover loans, MIGA usually issues coverage to match the length of such loans. MIGA cannot terminate the contract unless the investor defaults on its contractual obligations to MIGA, but the investor may reduce or cancel coverage without penalty on any contract anniversary date starting with the third anniversary.

2.8. Premium[170]

MIGA prices its guarantee premiums based on a calculation of both country and project risk. Fees average is approximately one percent of the insured amount per year, but can be significantly lower or higher.

3. Private insurance schemes

Since the early 1700s there have been insurers like Lloyd's, who have covered war perils as part of marine risk coverage. However, coverage of land-based war risk had been virtually nonexistent since World War II. But the magnitude of losses that could result from modern warfare made the private insurance market to insure also risks like nationalization, currency inconvertibility, war and political violence, terrorism, and contract cancellation.

Private insurance schemes are attractive for investors who cannot take advantage of MIGA. Furthermore, the range of possible risks that can be covered is much bigger (e.g.,

---

[169] Cf. https://www.miga.org/terms-conditions.
[170] https://www.miga.org/terms-conditions.

kidnap/ransom/extortion insurances). However, the premiums are substantially higher than the ones of MIGA and the duration of the insurance is often not as long as the period of the investment project.

VI. Unification of commercial law for international trade and cross border investments

1. Generally

International trade and cross border investments by companies have an important impact not just on the wealth of developed but also developing countries. Cross-border transactions and investments require the conclusion of various contracts like the sale of goods, financing, transport etc. Nevertheless, contracts do not necessarily settle all issues. They may lead to disputes and finally to the resolution of them. Therefore, it is important for the parties to know their mutual rights and obligations. Thus, international agreements help to figure out the applicable law based on uniform commercial law texts and conventions.

2. Organizations/Commissions

There are four organizations/commissions, which try to facilitate international trade and cross border investments from a legal point of view:

- *United Nations Commission on International Trade Law (UNCITRAL)*: The United Nations Commission on International Trade Law (UNCITRAL) was established by the General Assembly in 1966 (Resolution 2205 (XXI) of December 17, 1966). In establishing the commission, the General Assembly recognized that disparities in national laws governing international trade created obstacles to the flow of trade, and it regarded the commission as the vehicle by which the United Nations could play a more active role in reducing or removing these obstacles.[171]

- *International Institute for the Unification of Private Law (UNIDROIT)*: The International Institute for the Unification of Private Law (UNIDROIT) is an independent intergovernmental Organization with its

---

[171] Cf. https://uncitral.un.org/en/about.

seat in the Villa Aldobrandini in Rome. Its purpose is to study needs and methods for modernizing, harmonizing and coordinating private and in particular commercial law as between states and groups of states and to formulate uniform law instruments, principles and rules to achieve those objectives.[172] Probably the most important result of the UNIDROIT's work are the UNIDROIT Principles of International Commercial Contracts that are often used in interpretation of international commercial contracts or sometimes even chosen by the parties as the law applicable to the contract.

- *Hague Conference on Private International Law (Hague Conference)*: The Hague Conference on private international law is an intergovernmental organization with the purpose *"to work for the progressive unification of the rules of private international law"* (Article 1 of the Statutes). Since 1951, the Conference adopted over 40 international conventions, the practical operation of many of which is regularly reviewed by special commissions. Even when they are not ratified, the conventions have an influence upon legal systems, in both member and non-member states. They also form a source of inspiration for efforts to unify private international law at the regional level, for example within the Organization of American States or the European Union.[173]

- *World Trade Organization (WTO)*: The WTO is a global trade organization[174] with the aim of setting the rules and principles for trade between nations. Although the addressees are not directly private parties, but states, its importance is in providing for fundamental principles for multilateral trade and thereby has major impact also on contracts between private parties.

---

[172] Cf. https://www.unidroit.org/about-unidroit/overview.
[173] Cf. https://www.hcch.net/en/about.
[174] As of the beginning of 2022, WTO has 164 member states.

3. Conventions of importance for international trade and cross border business transactions

3.1. UN Convention on contracts for the international sale of goods (CISG)[175]

The United Nations Convention on Contracts for the International Sale of Goods (also called *"CISG"*) is a multilateral treaty that is a uniform international sales law, which has been prepared by UNCITRAL. The purpose of the CISG is to provide a modern, uniform and fair regime for contracts for the international sale of goods. As of the end of 2020, UNCITRAL and UN reported that 94 States have adopted the CISG. These states account for a significant proportion of world trade, making it one of the most successful international uniform laws. Initially it has been adopted by a diplomatic conference in 1980 and entered into force on January 1, 1988.

The contract of sale is the backbone of international trade in all countries, irrespective of their legal tradition or level of economic development. The CISG is therefore considered as one of the core international trade law conventions whose universal adoption is desirable.

The CISG is the result of a legislative effort that started at the beginning of the twentieth century. The resulting text provides a careful balance between the interests of the buyer and of the seller. It has also inspired contract law reforms at the national level.

The adoption of the CISG provides modern, uniform legislation for the international sale of goods that would apply whenever contracts for the sale of goods are concluded between parties with a place of business in contracting states. In these cases, the CISG would apply directly, avoiding recourse to rules of private international law to determine the law applicable to the contract, adding significantly to the certainty and predictability of international sales contracts.

---

[175] Cf. http://www.uncitral.org/uncitral/en/uncitral_texts/sale_goods/1980CISG.html.

Moreover, the CISG may apply to a contract for international sale of goods when the rules of private international law point at the law of a contracting state as the applicable one, or by virtue of the choice of the contractual parties, regardless of whether their places of business are located in a contracting state. In this latter case, the CISG provides a neutral body of rules that can be easily accepted in light of its transnational nature and of the wide availability of interpretative materials.

Finally, small and medium-sized enterprises as well as traders located in developing countries typically have reduced access to legal advice when negotiating a contract. Thus, they are more vulnerable to problems caused by inadequate treatment in the contract of issues relating to applicable law. The same enterprises and traders may also be the weaker contractual parties and could have difficulties in ensuring that the contractual balance is kept. Those merchants would therefore derive particular benefit from the default application of the fair and uniform regime of the CISG to contracts falling under its scope.

The CISG governs contracts for the international sales of goods between private businesses, excluding sales to consumers and sales of services, as well as sales of certain specified types of goods. Certain matters relating to the international sales of goods, for instance the validity of the contract and the effect of the contract on the property in the goods sold, fall outside the convention's scope. The second part of the CISG deals with the formation of the contract, which is concluded by the exchange of offer and acceptance. The third part of the CISG deals with the obligations of the parties to the contract. Obligations of the seller include delivering goods in conformity with the quantity and quality stipulated in the contract, as well as related documents, and transferring the property in the goods. Obligations of the buyer include payment of the price and taking delivery of the goods. In addition, this part provides common rules regarding remedies for breach of the contract. The aggrieved party may require performance, claim damages or avoid the contract in case of fundamental breach. Additional rules regulate passing of risk, anticipatory breach of contract, damages, and exemption from performance of the contract. Finally, while the CISG allows for freedom of form of the contract, states may lodge a declaration requiring the written form.

The CISG applies only to international transactions and avoids the recourse to rules of private international law for those contracts falling under its scope of application. International contracts falling outside the scope of application of the CISG, as well as contracts subject to a valid choice of other law, would not be affected by the CISG. Purely domestic sale contracts are not affected by the CISG and remain regulated by domestic law.

3.2. Convention on the limitation period in the international sale of goods[176]

The United Nations Convention on the Limitation Period in the International Sale of Goods (also *"Limitation Convention"*) is a uniform law treaty prepared by UNCITRAL, which deals with the prescription of actions relating to contracts for the international sale of goods due to the passage of time.

The Limitation Convention establishes uniform rules governing the period of time within which a party under a contract for the international sale of goods must commence legal proceedings against another party to assert a claim arising from the contract or relating to its breach, termination or validity. By doing so, it brings clarity and predictability on an aspect of great importance for the adjudication of the claim.

Most legal systems limit or prescribe a claim from being asserted after the lapse of a specified period of time to prevent the institution of legal proceedings at such a late date that the evidence relating to the claim is likely to be unreliable or lost and to protect against the uncertainty that would result if a party were to remain exposed to unasserted claims for an extensive period of time. However, numerous disparities exist among legal systems with respect to the conceptual basis for doing so, resulting in significant variations in the length of the limitation period and in the

---

[176] Cf. http://www.uncitral.org/uncitral/en/uncitral_texts/sale_goods/1974Convention_limitation_period.html.

rules governing the claims after that period. Those differences may create difficulties in the enforcement of claims arising from international sales transactions. In response to those difficulties, the Limitation Convention was prepared and adopted in 1974. The Limitation Convention was further amended by a protocol adopted in 1980 in order to harmonize its text with that of the CISG, in particular, with regard to scope of application and admissible declarations. Indeed, the Limitation Convention may be functionally seen as a part of the CISG and, as such, considered as an important step towards a comprehensive standardization of international sales law.

The limitation period is set at four years (article 8 of the Limitation Convention). A limitation period of four years' duration was thought to accomplish the aims of the limitation period and yet to provide an adequate period of time to enable a party to an international sales contract to assert his claim against the other party. Subject to certain conditions, that period may be extended to a maximum of ten years (article 23 of the Limitation Convention). With respect to the time when the limitation period commences to run, the basic rule is that it commences on the date on which the claim accrues. The convention establishes when claims for breach of contract, for defects in the goods or other lack of conformity and for fraud are deemed to accrue. Furthermore, this convention also regulates certain questions pertaining to the effect of commencing proceedings in a contracting state.

The Limitation Convention further provides rules on the cessation and extension of the limitation period. The period ceases when the claimant commences judicial or arbitral proceedings or when it asserts claims in an existing process. If the proceedings end without a binding decision on the merits, it is deemed that the limitation period continued to run during the proceedings. However, if the period has expired during the proceedings or has less than one year to run, the claimant is granted an additional year to commence new proceedings (article 17 of the Limitation Convention).

No claim shall be recognized or enforced in legal proceedings commenced after the expiration of the limitation period (article 25(1) of the Limitation Convention). Such expiration is not to be taken into consideration unless invoked by parties to the proceedings (article 24 of the Limitation Convention). However, states can make a declaration allowing courts to take into account the expiration of the limitation period on their own initiative (article 36 of the Limitation Convention). Otherwise, the only exception to the rule barring recognition and enforcement occurs when the party raises its claim as a defense to or set-off against a claim asserted by the other party (article 25(2) of the Limitation Convention).

The Limitation Convention applies only to international transactions and avoids the recourse to rules of private international law for those contracts falling under its scope of application. International contracts falling outside the scope of application of the Limitation Convention, as well as contracts subject to a valid choice of other law, would not be affected by the Limitation Convention. Purely domestic sales contracts are not affected by the Limitation Convention and are regulated by domestic law.

VII. Legal issues of cross-border joint ventures

1. Generally

A joint venture is a commercial arrangement between two or more independent parties in order to undertake economic activities together like developing and marketing products where the parties share risks, reduce costs and pool their resources, expertise, manufacturing know-how, marketing skills etc. to achieve a particular goal. Such joint ventures can be for one specific project only, or a continuing business relationship. They give each partner the opportunity to benefit significantly for the advantages of the other.[177] For example, in the oil and gas industry it is very common to form joint ventures.[178]

> **Example of a successful joint venture for manufacturing consumer electronics products in India**[179]
>
> A joint venture had brought together Indian and American partners to manufacture a specific consumer electronics product by a new legal entity in India. It was agreed that the Indian partner was responsible not only for manufacturing high-quality products, but also for marketing and distribution channel development, while the American partner supplied product and process technologies. The joint venture has been very successful and therefore the question of exporting these products came up. The partners would have to start to discuss whether exporting would meet their strategic goals and eventually how to proceed.

---

[177] Cf. also FRÉDÉRIC PREVOT/PIERRE-XAVIER MESCHI, Evolution of an international joint venture: the case of a French – Brazilian joint venture, in: Thunderbird International Business Review, Vol. 48(3) (2006), pp. 297 et seq.
[178] Cf. UNITED NATIONS CONFERENCE ON TRADE AND DEVELOPMENT, Word investment report 2007, Transnational corporations, extractive industries and development (2007), p. 159.
[179] ROBERT MILLER/JACK GLEN/FRED JASPERSEN/YANNIS KARMOKOLIAS, International joint ventures in developing countries, in: Finance & Development (March 1997), p. 28.

2. Types of joint ventures

There are the following types of joint ventures:

2.1. Contractual joint venture

Contractual joint ventures are joint business undertakings based on an agreement between two or more natural persons or companies who combine their efforts and resources in order to achieve some specific goal without establishing a separate company. Usually, such agreements are made for short- to medium-term alliances or for time-limited projects (e.g., in the field of civil engineering, and the construction, building and equipment supply industries).[180]

2.2. Equity joint venture

An equity joint venture is based on an agreement between two or more natural persons or companies to enter for a long-term duration into a separate business venture together. The business structure for an equity joint venture is a separate company, which is usually incorporated in the host state.[181]

3. Reasons for a joint venture

Some countries require foreign investors to form joint ventures with domestic companies or natural persons in order to enter the domestic market in the host state. In some jurisdictions, joint ventures must take a certain form. In other jurisdictions, joint ventures may be organized in accordance with a range of different structures. For example, Brazilian legislation has not expressly regulated joint

---

[180] Contractual joint ventures are often also called cooperative joint ventures or non-corporate joint ventures. Cf. YADONG LUO, Multinational enterprises in emerging markets (2002), p. 215 and KARL F. KREUZER, Legal aspects of international joint ventures in agriculture, pp. 2-3 and 8.
[181] Cf. KREUZER, op. cit., pp. 2-3 and 6-7.

ventures and thus not established a special treatment for this kind of arrangements. However, Brazilian law provides for several forms of business organizations, such as general partnerships, limited partnerships, limited companies and joint stock companies. Moreover, parties incorporating a joint venture company usually execute a shareholders' or a quotaholders' agreement (depending on the form of business organization being incorporated).[182]

The requirement to set up a company in the host state has in principle[183] not to be seen negatively as the establishment of a joint venture offers advantages to both the investor and the host state:[184]

> The principal advantages for the investor are:
> 1. Safeguarding or expanding of markets (instead of exports);
> 2. Risk sharing (the investor can share costs associated with marketing, product development, and other expenses, and thus reducing the financial burden);
> 3. Security of supply (raw materials);
> 4. Local marketing know-how;
> 5. Contacts with local banks and public authorities;
> 6. In certain political, social or economic circumstances it may be the only way to invest in a foreign country, gain new markets or defend or expand acquired markets;
> 7. Sharing of capital costs; and
> 8. Low labor and transport costs.

---

[182] Cf. GUILHERME LEITE/TALITA ALVES RODRIGUES, Brazil, in: International joint ventures, the comparative law yearbook of international business, Special issue, edited by Dennis Campbell (2008), pp. 3-4.

[183] However, any special requirements for foreign investments like the necessity that in order to make the investment the foreign investor has to set up a particular legal form, is a restriction on the party autonomy and thus an exception to this basic legal principle.

[184] Cf. AIMIN YAN/YADONG LUO, International joint ventures, theory and practice (2001), pp. 112-113 and MAMARINTA P. MABABYA, The role of multinational companies in the middle east: the case of Saudi Arabia (2002), pp. 179-180 and the list made by KREUZER, op. cit., pp. 5-6.

The principal advantages for the home state are:
1. Foreign exchange earnings through capital import and commodity export;
2. Acquisition of new technology (a joint venture allows very often an access to new technology; sharing innovative and proprietary technology can improve products, as well as the understanding of technological processes);
3. Acquisition of technical skills;
4. Acquisition of management know-how;
5. Import substitution;
6. Creation of employment; and
7. Utilization and processing of local resources for export.

4. Joint venture agreement

4.1. Generally

Regardless of the type of joint venture, which has been chosen by the parties, and the fact that there is no limit to the matters that can be covered in a joint venture agreement, a clear agreement is essential for building a good relationship. Thus, the parties should consider including at least the following points in a joint venture agreement.[185]

4.2. Definitions

It is common to start such agreements with the definitions. They usually cover the parties etc.

---

[185] Cf. for example also the checklist for a model joint venture agreement by the American Bar Association (https://apps.americanbar.org/buslaw/newsletter/0049/materials/book.pdf) and ALAN S. GUTTERMAN, A short course in international joint ventures, how to negotiate, establish and manage an international joint venture (2009), pp. 13 et seq.

4.3. Objective of the joint venture

A joint venture agreement should include a section at the beginning covering the scope/purpose of the joint venture. Not only is this sometimes a matter of local law, but it is often essential to make sure both parties are clear on the scope and scale of the joint venture's operations. This will help when the agreement and the genuine will of the parties have to be interpreted, which may be important in case of a dispute. Thus, it has to be held what activities the joint venture does expressly intend to do.

4.4. Contributions of the parties

The parties usually list their contributions (and the liability for the contributions) regarding the joint venture.

Possible contributions of a foreign investor are:
- technical skills and know how,
- patents,
- marketing techniques,
- production techniques,
- specialized personnel, and/or
- financial resources.

Possible contributions of a domestic partner are:
- real estate,
- existing production facilities,
- capital,
- environmental knowledge,
- supplier, labor, customer contacts, and/or
- social and political goodwill.

4.5. Organization and management of the joint venture

The agreement has to address what kind of organization will be formed. If it is necessary to use a corporate vehicle for the joint venture, then the joint venture agreement should define the form of the legal entity. The joint ventures' governance structure will depend largely on the actual structure chosen.

4.6. New parties

The agreement has to contain clauses, which explain how will be dealt with possible new partners. Usually new partners are just allowed when both parties accept the new partners. Furthermore, such agreements contain requirements/prohibitions regarding the sale of the shares or quotas of the joint venture legal entity.

4.7. Termination of the joint venture

The termination provisions for a joint venture belong to the most important terms of the entire document. The agreement would typically provide for termination due to a breach of the agreement by the other party, or if one of the parties goes into bankruptcy, or if there is a change of control of one of the parties. The termination provisions might also cover the termination of the joint venture in the event of expropriation of the joint venture's assets.

4.8. Choice-of-law-clause

Many national jurisdictions allow the parties of a joint venture to choose the applicable law to their contractual relationship. Thus, it is important that the parties to a joint venture agreement choose and specify the governing law.

4.9. Dispute resolution mechanism

The agreement should contain clauses, with which the parties choose a dispute resolution mechanism (e.g., arbitration proceedings shall be conducted under the rules of UNCITRAL etc.).

Example: Egypt to pay Spanish-Italian joint venture in natural gas dispute[186]

A joint venture between Spain's Naturgy and Italy's Eni has been awarded a USD 2 billion settlement from Egypt over gas supplies by a World Bank arbitration body, in a move that could accelerate the resumption of the country's liquefied natural gas exports. The ruling by the International Centre for Settlement of Investment Disputes (ICSID) comes after Egypt stopped supplying gas to Unión Fenosa Gas joint venture's Damietta LNG plant as the country faced internal energy shortages in the wake of a domestic political turmoil. Unión Fenosa Gas took its case to the ICSID in 2014. The arbitration body found that in stopping the gas supply Egypt had failed to grant Unión Fenosa Gas *"fair and equitable treatment"*, contravening the country's bilateral investment protection treaty with Spain.

5. Tax issues

Very often tax issues that arise from the establishment, operation and termination of a joint venture have an impact on the choice between the aforementioned types of vehicles. Thus, it is important that either the foreign investor as well as the joint venture partner in the host state verify the respective taxation in each state. It is noteworthy that some states give unilateral tax reductions/exemptions for joint ventures. Furthermore, the parties of a joint venture should also consult the BITs, MITs or double taxation agreements in order to avoid double taxation issues.[187]

6. Competition law issues

In principle, cooperation of undertakings, in spite of their positive effects, might raise concerns of competition authorities since such a cooperation could increase the risk

---

[186] Cf. MYLES MCCORMICK/DAVID SHEPPARD, Egypt to pay Spanish-Italian JV $2bn in natural gas dispute, in: Financial Times (September 3, 2018).
[187] Cf. GUTTERMAN, Joint Ventures, p. 20.

of anticompetitive behavior of the undertakings concerned; instead of competing between themselves, which would be a logical and natural behavior on the market, undertakings become business partners and consequently are not competitors. This might ultimately be detrimental for consumers. Whether there really are competition concerns resulting from a particular joint venture shall depend on all the circumstances of the case, but these issues should never be neglected.

VIII. Corporate social responsibility (CSR) and international investments

1. Generally

Corporate social responsibility (CSR) in relation to international acting companies can be defined as their contribution through their business activities in order to achieve a sustainable development in host states. Taking into account CSR issues like working conditions, human rights, environment, anti-corruption measures, fair competition, consumer interests, taxes, transparency, gender equality etc. does not just support and improve a sustainable development or maximize the positive societal outcome of investments as well as business activities in the host state, but also help to achieve a bigger economic growth and a safer investment environment with a lower risk of nationalizations.

Various BITs and MITs reflect CSR issues. It is noteworthy that the inclusion of CSR concepts and principles in trade and investment agreements are considered as an opportunity for achieving greater coherence in CSR by providing signals to companies about which guidelines, standards and labels to adopt. For example, some of these agreements provide for the establishment of a committee on investments that will host a forum to promote co-operation and facilitate joint initiatives on CSR. This type of formal networks helps to promote CSR coherence.

Canada - Peru Free Trade Agreement
Chapter Eight - Investment
Section A - Substantive Obligations

Article 809: Health, Safety and Environmental Measures

The Parties recognize that it is inappropriate to encourage investment by relaxing domestic health, safety or environmental measures. Accordingly, a Party should not waive or otherwise derogate from, or offer to waive or otherwise derogate from, such measures as an encouragement for the establishment, acquisition, expansion or retention in its territory of an investment of an investor.

If a Party considers that the other Party has offered such an encouragement, it may request consultations with the other Party and the two Parties shall consult with a view to avoiding any such encouragement.

Article 810: Corporate Social Responsibility

Each Party should encourage enterprises operating within its territory or subject to its jurisdiction to voluntarily incorporate internationally recognized standards of corporate social responsibility in their internal policies, such as statements of principle that have been endorsed or are supported by the Parties. These principles address issues such as labor, the environment, human rights, community relations and anti-corruption. The Parties remind those enterprises of the importance of incorporating such corporate social responsibility standards in their internal policies.

Article 817: Committee on Investment

The Parties hereby establish a Committee on Investment, comprising representatives of each Party.

The Committee shall provide a forum for the Parties to consult on issues related to this Chapter that are referred to it by a Party. The Committee shall meet at such times as agreed by the Parties and should work to promote cooperation and facilitate joint initiatives, which may address issues such as corporate social responsibility and investment facilitation.

Furthermore, not just host states, but also the home states of foreign investors enacted national legislations which force a foreign investor to take CSR issues into account for his investment in a host state.

2. Benefits of CSR[188]

For example, international acting companies benefit from taking into account CSR issues as follows:

---

[188] Cf. https://www.seco.admin.ch/seco/en/home/Aussenwirtschafts politik_Wirtschaftliche_Zusammenarbeit/Wirtschaftsbeziehungen/

- By making savings in energy and raw material consumption thanks to more productive workers (e.g., reducing illness- and accident-related absences and early retirement from working life), one has better credit terms and easier access to the capital market, and companies benefit financially from CSR. A consistent CSR management can help companies to obtain a favorable market position, can boost innovation and avoid reputational threats.
- Respecting CSR can have a positive influence on companies as customers are increasingly taking CSR criteria into account.
- A reputation as a responsible employer also boosts recruitment and motivates employees.
- A responsible business conduct can give companies an advantage in public tenders as more and more governments of the host states require strict adherence to law provisions regarding employment conditions and equal pay.

Companies which take CSR issues into account can provide through their actions for the following positive societal outcome:

- Consistent and broad implementation of CSR do not just help to overcome social challenges in the host state (e.g., skills shortage, unemployment, balancing work and family), but also position the home state of the investor as a responsible economy.
- Respecting CSR issues helps to preserve natural resources, protect health and improve life quality.
- Many countries do not have adequate statutory provisions or do not implement these adequately, despite being responsible for developing and implementing the framework conditions for their own social and economic policies. If a company reduces the social and environmental risks in the host state, then this does not just improve the living conditions, but also the global sustainability.

Gesellschaftliche_Verantwortung_der_Unternehmen/Nutzen_der_CSR1.html.

3. International CSR standards

3.1. Generally

Recently, CSR has become more and more important on the international stage and undergone conceptual changes. New tools have been developed and existing ones updated and enhanced.

In order to achieve better protection of people and the environment, there are internationally recognized standards and guidelines, such as the UN Guiding Principles on Business and Human Rights, the OECD Declaration on international investment and multinational enterprises, ISO 26000 Guidance on social responsibility, ILO standards, etc. International plans and agreements, such as the Paris Agreement, Sustainable Development Goals (SDGs), Task Force on Climate-related Financial Disclosures (TCFD), UN Agreement on Transnational Corporations and Human Rights (Binding Treaty), are also intended to harmonize sustainability regulations for companies in order to achieve a sustainable development and to create a level playing field.

3.2. OECD Declaration on international investment and multinational enterprises

The OECD aims to enhance the contribution of international investment to growth and sustainable development worldwide by advancing investment policy reform and international co-operation. First adopted in 1976, the OECD Declaration on international investment and multinational enterprises is a policy commitment by adhering governments to provide an open and transparent environment for international investments and to encourage the positive contribution multinational enterprises can make to economic and social progress. All parts of the Declaration are subject to periodical reviews. All 36 OECD countries, and 13 non-OECD countries[189] have subscribed to the Declaration.

The Declaration consists of four elements:

---

[189] Argentina, Brazil, Bulgaria, Croatia, Egypt, Jordan, Kazakhstan, Morocco, Peru, Romania, Tunisia, Ukraine and Uruguay.

- *Guidelines for Multinational Enterprises*: The Guidelines for Multinational Enterprises[190] are recommendations on responsible business conduct addressed by governments to multinational enterprises operating in or from adhering countries. Observance of the Guidelines is supported by a unique implementation mechanism. Adhering governments – through their network of National Contact Points (NCP)[191] – are responsible for promoting the Guidelines and helping to resolve issues that arise under the specific instance procedures. Any suspected breach against the OECD guidelines can be reported to the NCPs, which offer a platform for dialogue or a mediation procedure. Sector-specific guidelines (covering minerals, agriculture, textiles, finance, etc.)[192] support the implementation of the OECD guidelines and enterprises' due diligence in particular.
- *National Treatment*: A voluntary undertaking by adhering countries to accord to foreign-controlled enterprises on their territories a treatment no less favourable than that accorded in like situations to domestic enterprises.
- *Conflicting requirements*: Adhering countries shall co-operate in order to avoid or minimize the imposition of conflicting requirements on multinational enterprises.
- *International investment incentives and disincentives*: Adhering countries recognise the need to give due weight to the interest of adhering countries affected by laws and practices in this field; they will endeavour to make measures as transparent as possible.

3.3. UN Guiding Principles on Business and Human Rights

The UN Guiding Principles on Business and Human Rights[193] include 31 principles and are based on three pillars:

---

[190] Cf. http://mneguidelines.oecd.org/.
[191] Cf. http://mneguidelines.oecd.org/ncps/.
[192] Cf. http://mneguidelines.oecd.org/sectors/.
[193] Cf. https://www.ohchr.org/Documents/Publications/GuidingPrinciples BusinessHR_EN.pdf.

- *State duty to protect human rights*: Countries must take the necessary measures (e.g., laws, incentives and awareness raising) in order to protect the population from human rights abuses.
- *Corporate responsibility*: Legal entities must act with due diligence in order to avoid infringing the rights of others and to address any negative impacts. The UN principles hold that legal entities have the power to affect all of the internationally recognized rights. Thus, there is a responsibility of both the state and the private sector to acknowledge their respective roles in upholding and protecting human rights.
- *Access to remedy*: Countries and legal entities have a responsibility to facilitate effective remediation for those affected by means of judicial and extrajudicial measures.

The principles can be applied to all countries and legal entities regardless of their size, sector, location or ownership and organizational structures. However, they do not constitute international obligations.

3.4. UN Global Compact

Launched in 2000, the United Nations Global Compact (UNGC)[194] is a call to legal entities to align strategies and operations with universal principles on human rights, labor, environment and anti-corruption, and take actions that advance societal goals. Today, hundreds of companies and non-profit organizations from all regions of the world, are engaged in the UN Global Compact, working to advance 10 Universal Principles in the areas of human rights, labor, the environment and anti-corruption.

THE 10 PRINCIPLES:

HUMAN RIGHTS

1. Businesses should support and respect the protection of internationally proclaimed human rights; and

---

[194] Cf. https://www.globalcompact.ch/ungc.

2. Make sure that they are not complicit in human rights abuses.

LABOR
3. Businesses should uphold the freedom of association and the effective recognition of the right to collective bargaining;
4. The elimination of all forms of forced and compulsory labor;
5. The effective abolition of child labor; and
6. The elimination of discrimination in respect of employment and occupation.

ENVIRONMENT
7. Businesses should support a precautionary approach to environmental challenges;
8. Undertake initiatives to promote greater environmental responsibility; and
9. Encourage the development and diffusion of environmentally friendly technologies.

ANTI-CORRUPTION
10. Businesses should work against all forms of corruption, including extortion and bribery.

Once a signatory to the UN Global Compact, organizations are expected to:

- set in motion changes to their operations in order to implement the 10 principles;
- publicly advocate the Global Compact and its principles via communications vehicles such as press releases, speeches, etc.;
- business participants must publish an annual Communication on Progress (COP) that describes the ways in which the business supports the Global Compact and its 10 principles; and
- non business participants must publish an annual Communication on Engagement (COE) that describes the ways in which the organization supports the Global Compact and its 10 principles.

3.5. ISO 26000 Guidance on Social Responsibility

ISO 26000 – Guidance on social responsibility[195] provides guidance to all types of businesses and organizations, regardless of their size or location, on:

- concepts, terms and definitions related to social responsibility;
- the background, trends and characteristics of social responsibility;
- principles and practices relating to social responsibility;
- the core subjects and issues of social responsibility;
- integrating, implementing and promoting socially responsible behavior throughout the organization and, through its policies and practices, within its sphere of influence;
- identifying and engaging with stakeholders; and
- communicating commitments, performance and other information related to social responsibility.

ISO 26000 – Guidance on social responsibility is intended to assist businesses and organizations in contributing to sustainable development. It is intended to encourage them to go beyond legal compliance, recognizing that compliance with law is a fundamental duty of any organization and an essential part of their social responsibility. It is intended to promote common understanding in the field of social responsibility, and to complement other instruments and initiatives for social responsibility, not to replace them.

3.6. Global Reporting Initiative

The Global Reporting Initiative (GRI)[196] helps businesses and governments worldwide to understand and communicate their impact on critical sustainability issues such as climate change, human rights, governance and social well-being. This enables real action to create social, environmental and economic benefits for everyone. The GRI Sustainability

---

[195] Cf. https://www.iso.org/iso-26000-social-responsibility.html.
[196] Cf. https://www.globalreporting.org.

Reporting Standards are developed with true multi-stakeholder contributions and rooted in the public interest.

3.7. ILO-Standards

Since 1919, the International Labor Organization (ILO) has brought together governments, employers and workers from 187 member states to set labor standards, develop policies and programs to promote decent work for all women and men.

The ILO Declaration on Fundamental Principles and Rights at Work, adopted in 1998, is intended to promote the universal application of rights recognized as fundamental by all ILO member states. Fundamental rights and principles at work are considered universal minimum social requirements. For this reason, there are numerous references to these fundamental principles and rights.

The fundamental principles and rights at work have been expressed and developed in the form of specific rights and obligations in the ILO Conventions recognized as fundamental. All ILO member states undertake to respect, promote and implement the fundamental principles and rights at work in good faith. This is irrespective of whether they have ratified the relevant conventions or not.

At its June 2022 session, the International Labor Conference (ILC) decided to amend the 1998 Declaration to add a safe and healthy working environment to the fundamental principles and rights at work. As a result, the Declaration now includes the following five fundamental principles and rights:

1. freedom of association and the effective recognition of the right to collective bargaining;
2. the elimination of all forms of forced or compulsory labor;
3. the effective abolition of child labor;
4. the elimination of discrimination in respect of employment and occupation;
5. a safe and healthy working environment.

3.8. 2030 Agenda for Sustainable Development (UN development goals)[197]

The 2030 Agenda for Sustainable Development (UN development goals)[198] was developed by the international community in 2015 in order to contribute to global development, promote human well-being and to protect the environment. The 17 Sustainable Development Goals and their 169 targets form a core element of this agenda.

3.9. EU Strategy for Corporate Social Responsibility[199]

The EU Strategy for Corporate Social Responsibility describes the EU's strategic approach and the specific measures it has in place regarding CSR. The European Commission believes that CSR is important for the sustainability, competitiveness, and innovation of EU legal entities and the EU economy. It brings benefits for risk management, cost savings, access to capital, customer relationships, and human resource management. Thus, the EU decided to amend accordingly various directives.

3.10. G7

Sustainability was also a key topic on the G7 Agenda 2022. Discussions are taking place in the G7 on the introduction of an internationally binding instrument for globally sustainable corporate due diligence or on sustainable supply chains. Such an internationally binding instrument would not only better protect people and the environment in global supply chains and improve access to justice for those affected by human rights abuses and corporate pollution. The agreement would also create a level playing field and legal certainty for companies worldwide.

---

[197] https://sustainabledevelopment.un.org/post2015/transformingourworld.
[198] https://sustainabledevelopment.un.org/post2015/transformingourworld.
[199] Cf. http://ec.europa.eu/growth/industry/corporate-social-responsibility/.

3.11. TCFD

The Task Force on Climate-related Financial Disclosures (TCFD) was established at the end of 2015 by the Financial Stability Board (FSB) in order to develop recommendations on corporate financial transparency in relation to climate risks. Its recommendations provide a common international framework that allows companies, as well as financial industry actors, to properly assess and price their exposure to climate concerns in order to implement the necessary strategies in their business operations.

More broadly, the goal is to make markets more efficient and economies better equipped to deal with climate change. The task force's recommendations are organized into four themes: (i) *Governance*: information on the governance of the organization's management of climate-related risks and opportunities; (ii) *Strategy*: information on the effective and potential climate-related risks and opportunities on the organization's business, strategy and financial planning, where material; (iii) *Risk management*: information on how the organization identifies, assesses and manages climate-related risks; (iv) *Metrics and targets*: Information on which metrics and targets are used to assess and manage relevant climate-related risks and opportunities, if material.

3.12. Paris Agreement

The Paris Agreement, often referred to as the Paris Accords or the Paris Climate Accords, is an international treaty on climate change and a legally binding instrument under the United Nations Framework Convention on Climate Change (UNFCCC). It contains elements for the successive reduction of global greenhouse gas emissions and is based for the first time on common principles for all states: Among other things, the Paris Agreement aims to limit average global warming to well below 2°C compared to pre-industrial times, with a maximum temperature increase of 1.5°C.

For example, it is also worth mentioning that Switzerland is committed under the Paris Climate Agreement to reduce its emissions by 50 percent by 2030 compared to 1990

(Nationally Determined Contribution, NDC). This is to be achieved in part through climate protection projects abroad. The Paris Climate Agreement allows for such bi- or plurilateral cooperation. For this purpose, Switzerland concludes bilateral treaties. The international treaties regulate the framework conditions of the cooperation and clarify the requirements for the recognition of the international transfer of emission reductions by the contracting parties. Thus, the agreements create the legal framework for commercial contracts between sellers and buyers of emission reductions. Under the agreements, only emission reductions are recognized where there is no evidence of human rights violations in the implementation of the climate protection projects approved under the agreement (as well as no corruption in relation to these same climate protection projects). The project owners (mostly private carbon offset project offices such as Myclimate or South Pole) must submit complete monitoring reports to the federal government and the government of the partner country. In addition, third parties can report human rights violations to Switzerland, which then has the possibility to unilaterally stop the recognition of emission reductions from the projects in question.

3.13. UN Convention on Transnational Corporations and Human Rights

In 2014, the United Nations Human Rights Council (UNHRC) adopted a resolution to establish an intergovernmental working group to develop a legally binding international instrument on corporations and human rights. Since 2015, eight sessions of the working group have been held at the United Nations. At its last meeting in October 2022, a third revised version of the draft treaty was negotiated in Geneva. The draft stipulates that the future treaty will apply to human rights violations related to all economic activities, especially transnational ones. Victims must have access to the courts of the country where the violations occurred or to the courts of the country where the responsible company is based. States must enact laws that require transnationally active companies to fulfill due diligence obligations to prevent the negative impact of their activities on human rights.

Switzerland has followed the discussions without a negotiating mandate from the beginning as an observer and has contributed with clarifying questions. It gives priority to the implementation of the UN Guiding Principles on Business and Human Rights adopted by the UNHRC in 2011 and the aforementioned OECD Guidelines for Multinational Enterprises.

The European Union has so far taken a position of *"partial engagement"* with no negotiation date for the text of the draft treaty. A handful of EU member states have adopted binding laws on business and human rights, such as France.

3.14. Unidroit

Unidroit, the international organization for the unification of private law with around 70 member states, decided in 2022 to start work in the area of corporate responsibility during the 2023-2025 work program. The focus will be on the duties of care voluntarily and contractually agreed upon by companies vis-à-vis their suppliers; the issue of liability will not be the subject of the work.

4. Multinational legislation

4.1. Generally

The EU recently revised and amended Directive 2013/34/EU, Directive 2004/109/EC, Directive 2006/43/EC and Regulation (EU) No. 537/2014 with regard to corporate sustainability reporting (so-called "*Corporate Sustainability Reporting Directive*").[200] These changes have been adopted and entered into force in January 2023.

In addition, the EU is currently drafting a Directive on corporate sustainability due diligence (so-called "*Corporate*

---

[200] Cf. https://eur-lex.europa.eu/legal-content/EN/TXT/HTML/?uri=CELEX:52021PC0189&from=DE.

Sustainability Due Dilligence Directive").[201] The importance of this legislation should not be underestimated as many countries like Switzerland have an internationally coordinated legislation that is primarily based on the directives and regulations currently in force in the EU.[202]

4.2. Corporate Sustainability Due Diligence Directive

4.2.1. Generally

On February 23, 2022, the European Commission presented a proposal for a Corporate Sustainability Due Diligence Directive (CS3D). After several setbacks and deliberations, the European Parliament approved on April 24, 2024 with 374 votes against 235 and 19 abstentions the new "due diligence" directive, agreed on with the Council, requiring firms and their upstream and downstream partners, including supply, production and distribution to prevent, end or mitigate their adverse impact on human rights and the environment. Such impact will include slavery, child labor, labor exploitation, biodiversity loss, pollution or destruction of natural heritage.

The Council has formally adopted CS3D on May 24, 2024. This was the last step in the decision-making procedure and the directive introduces obligations for large companies regarding adverse impacts of their activities on human rights and environmental protection. It also lays down the liabilities linked to these obligations. The rules concern not only the companies' operations, but also the activities of their subsidiaries, and those of their business partners along the companies' chain of activities.

---

[201] https://commission.europa.eu/business-economy-euro/doing-business-eu/corporate-sustainability-due-diligence_en.

[202] Report of the Swiss Federal Department of Justice, Swiss Federal Office of Justice on the 'Draft Sustainability Obligations EU' and applicable law Switzerland, November 25, 2022, p. 4 (REPORT EU/SWITZERLAND-STAINABILITY OBLIGATIONS).

4.2.2. Scope of application, risk-based approach and transition plan

The rules of this Directive will apply to EU companies and parent companies with over 1000 employees and a worldwide turnover higher than 450 million euro. It will also apply to companies with franchising or licensing agreements in the EU ensuring a common corporate identity with worldwide turnover higher than 80 million euro if at least 22.5 million euro was generated by royalties. Non-EU companies, parent companies and companies with franchising or licensing agreements in the EU reaching the same turnover thresholds in the EU will also be covered.

4.2.3. Due diligence obligations

These companies will have to integrate due diligence into their policies, make related investments, seek contractual assurances from their partners, improve their business plan or provide support to small and medium-sized business partners to ensure they comply with new obligations. Companies will also have to adopt a transition plan to make their business model compatible with the Paris Agreement global warming limit of 1.5°C.

4.2.4. Fines and compensation of victims

Member states will be required to provide companies with detailed online information on their due diligence obligations via practical portals containing the Commission's guidance.

They will also create or designate a supervisory authority to investigate and impose penalties on non-complying firms. These will include "naming and shaming" and fines of up to 5% of companies' net worldwide turnover.

The Commission will establish the European Network of Supervisory Authorities to support cooperation and enable exchange of best practices.

Furthermore, companies will be liable for damages caused by breaching their due diligence obligations and will have to fully compensate their victims.

4.3. Corporate Sustainability Reporting Directive

4.3.1. Generally

On April 21, 2021, the European Commission presented a proposal for a directive amending the directives and the regulation regarding corporate sustainability reporting. The Council of Ministers agreed on a common position on February 24, 2022. It proposed an amendment to the scope proposed by the European Commission, with certain alleviations of reporting requirements for listed SMEs. On June 21, 2022, the Council and the European Parliament reached a preliminary agreement on new rules for corporate sustainability reporting. The European Parliament adopted it on November 10, 2022, by 525 votes to 60. Thereinafter, the EU policymakers reached an agreement on the Corporate Sustainability Reporting Directive that came into force 20 days after its publication in the EU Office Journal (December 16, 2022). It brings sustainability reporting to the same level as financial reporting for the first time ever. This is fundamental to support the EU Green Deal's ambitions and to transform Europe into the first climate neutral economy by 2050. The directive is applicable starting from:
- January 1, 2024 for companies already subject to the directive on the disclosure of non-financial information;
- January 1, 2025 for large companies not currently subject to the Non-Financial Information Directive;
- January 1, 2026 for listed SMEs and small and non-complex credit institutions and captive insurance companies.

The Corporate Sustainability Reporting Directive aims to amend four existing pieces of legislation: The Accounting Directive (EU Directive 2014/95 and EU Directive 2013/34), the Statutory Audit Directive (EU Directive 2006/43), the Statutory Audit Regulation (EU Regulation 537/2014) and the Transparency Directive (EU Directive 2004/109). The adjustments are made in accordance with the

Regulation of November 27, 2019 on sustainability-related disclosure requirements in the financial services sector (EU Regulation 2019/2088, so-called *"Disclosure Directive"*) and the Regulation of June 18, 2020 on the establishment of a framework to facilitate sustainable investment and amending EU Regulation (EU) 2019/2088 (so-called *"Taxonomy Directive"* [EU Regulation 2020/852]). The coherence between sustainability reporting requirements and comparability are to be improved. According to the Corporate Sustainability Reporting Directive, the following innovations are envisaged: (i) The extension of the scope of application of the reporting obligations to further companies, including all large companies and listed companies, with the exception of listed micro-enterprises (newly, around 49,000 companies would be covered, previously there were approx. 11,600) and non-EU companies (companies from third countries operating in the EU) above certain thresholds; (ii) the requirement for external verification of sustainability reporting (in the management report); (iii) more detailed disclosures on the information to be provided by companies and the requirement for reporting in line with the mandatory EU-wide sustainability reporting standards (in the management report); (iv) ensuring that all information is published as part of the companies' management reports and in a digital, machine-readable format.[203]

4.3.2. New terminology

As requested by various stakeholders, the term *"sustainability information"* is used in the Corporate Sustainability Reporting Directive instead of the term *"non-financial information"* and the terminology is also changed accordingly in EU Directive 2013/34. This is intended to take into account the fact that information on sustainability is increasingly of financial relevance. Furthermore, the following newly used terms are defined: *"sustainability aspects"*, *"sustainability reporting"*, *"intangible assets"* and *"independent assurance provider"*.

---

[203] REPORT EU/SWITZERLAND-STAINABILITY OBLIGATIONS, pp. 8-9.

4.3.3. Scope of application

The following companies in particular are covered by the scope of application:

- *Large EU companies* that meet at least two of the following three criteria: More than 250 employees; more than EUR 40 million in sales revenue; more than EUR 20 million in total assets.
- *Companies listed* on *regulated markets in the EU*.
- *SMEs listed in the EU* that meet at least two of the following three criteria: a maximum of 50 employees, a maximum of EUR 8 million in sales revenue and a maximum of EUR 4 million in total assets. The special features of SMEs will be taken into account. They will be able to take advantage of an exemption (*"opting-out"*) during a transitional period, i.e., they will be exempt from the application of the directive until 2028. *Exempt* are *EU micro-enterprises* that meet at least two of the following three criteria: maximum 10 employees; maximum of EUR 700,000 turnover and maximum of EUR 350,000 balance sheet total.
- *Companies from third countries* that generate *net sales of more than EUR 150 million in the EU* and *have at least one subsidiary or branch in the EU* must submit a report, limited to their so-called ESG impacts, i.e., on environmental, social and governance aspects within the meaning of the directive (from 2028 onwards).

4.3.4. Clarification of the so-called "dual materiality"

The existing principle of *"dual materiality"* is clarified in the Corporate Sustainability Reporting Directive. Companies are now obliged to report both on how sustainability aspects affect their business results, their situation and their business performance (*"outside-in perspective"*) and on how these aspects affect people and the environment (*"inside-out perspective"*).

4.3.5. More detailed disclosures on the nature of information

The management report must include *"information"* that is necessary for an understanding of the sustainability impacts of the company's activities and the effects of sustainability issues on the company's business performance, results of operations and position. They must include forward-looking, retrospective, qualitative and quantitative disclosures.

These disclosures include, in particular, the following:
- Description of the business model (including a description of its compatibility with the goal of limiting global warming to 1.5°C);
- Description of sustainability goals;
- Description of the role of the administrative, management and supervisory bodies in connection with sustainability aspects;
- Description of sustainability policy;
- Description of due diligence processes implemented with regard to sustainability aspects;
- Description of the most significant actual or potential negative impacts in the supply chain (including own operations, its products and services, its business relationships and its supply chain);
- Description of the measures taken to prevent, mitigate or remedy negative impacts and the success of these measures;
- Description of the most important risks in connection with sustainability aspects;
- Identification of indicators relevant to the aforementioned items to be disclosed;
- Information on intangible assets (intellectual capital, human capital, etc.).

The companies report the aforementioned information in accordance with the EU-wide standards for sustainability reporting according to the Corporate Sustainability Reporting Directive.

Furthermore, companies are now required to disclose information on their strategy, objectives, the role of the board of directors and management, material negative impacts related to the company and its supply chain, intangible assets, as well as information on how they have determined the information to be provided (article 1 para. 3 Corporate Sustainability Reporting Directive).

4.3.6. Standards for sustainability reporting

The EU Commission is newly empowered under the Reporting Directive to adopt EU-wide standards for sustainability reporting (standards for specific sectors, etc.), subject to a specific procedure (consultation of various stakeholders, etc.) (article 1 para. 3, para. 4 and para. 11 Corporate Sustainability Reporting Directive).

A key element of the Directive is to require certain categories of companies to provide information according to these mandatory standards in order to ensure the comparability and relevance of this information. The EU Commission will adopt standards for large companies and separate, proportionate standards for SMEs. The standards will cover the information to be disclosed on *"environmental factors"* (climate change, resources, biodiversity, ecosystems), *"social factors"* (gender equality, equal pay, working conditions, respect for human rights, fundamental freedoms, democratic principles and standards), and *"governance factors"* (role and composition of the company's administrative, management and supervisory bodies, business ethics [including anti-corruption, anti-bribery], and the use of financial instruments).

The EU Commission is authorized to determine the procedure for establishing the equivalence of standards used by third countries outside of the EU (article 2 para. 3 Corporate Sustainability Reporting Directive).

4.3.7. External verification of sustainability reporting

The requirement for an external audit of sustainability information has been introduced (article 1 para. 10 Corporate Sustainability Reporting Directive). The subject matter of this audit is described in article 1 para. 10 and article 2 para. 1 Corporate Sustainability Reporting Directive and the requirements for it are stated in article 3 para. 3 Corporate Sustainability Reporting Directive.

4.3.8. Mandatory reporting in the management report; uniform electronic reporting format

It is mandatory to implement the sustainability reporting in the management report, in a uniform electronic, digital reporting format; the management report and the audit opinion of the external auditor/the audit firm must be published (article 1 para. 4, para. 8 and para. 9 as well as article 3 para. 1 Corporate Sustainability Reporting Directive).

4.3.9. Sanctions

Article 1 para. 12 Corporate Sustainability Reporting Directive lists the possible sanctions: Public disclosure of those responsible and the nature of the violation, an order to cease and desist from repeating the conduct in violation of the rules and, finally, fines. Member states determine the type and level of sanctions, taking into account certain relevant circumstances such as the severity and duration of the violation, the degree of responsibility, the financial strength of the responsible parties, etc.

4.3.10 Diversity concept

The companies concerned must include a reference to gender in the description of the diversity concept pursued in connection with administrative, management and supervisory bodies (article 1 para. 5 Corporate Sustainability Reporting Directive).

4.4. Effects of the EU Corporate Sustainability Due Diligence and Reporting Directives on Companies from Non-EU Member States

The EU Directives (Corporate Sustainability Due Diligence Directive and Corporate Sustainability Reporting Directive) contain third country provisions, i.e., companies from third countries are covered by the scope of application if they meet the aforementioned requirements. Following issues have to be examined for each state separately in the view of their respective legislation: how many companies are affected, what do these changes mean in terms of the competitiveness and market environment of these companies, what will be the economic impact and which measures, if any, should be taken.

In the case of Switzerland, the impact of the new EU directives is not to be underestimated as they will impose additional efforts for Swiss companies – especially for SMEs. In addition, competitive disadvantages for Swiss suppliers of companies covered by the EU Directives in relation to competitors from the EU can be assumed. Since sales data of Swiss companies in the EU are not publicly available, no information can be given on the number of affected companies. This would require a detailed study, e.g., with company surveys.

IX. International insolvency law

1. Basics of international insolvency law

The economic relevance of insolvency law has become obvious in the recent financial crises (World Finance Crisis/Subprime Crisis, Euro Crisis, Corona Crisis, 2023 Banking Crisis etc.), in which even companies previously considered financially *"unsinkable"* have faltered (UBS), merged (CS into UBS) or even been completely liquidated (Lehman Brothers). In numerous cases, only a restructuring process with massive state aid (GM) prevented the liquidation of large companies. In view of the numerous headline-grabbing insolvencies of large companies, it is often forgotten that numerous small and medium-sized companies also got into financial difficulties in the course of a financial crisis. It is these cases of insolvency which, away from the media and political interest (and thus government bailout money), ultimately have the most serious impact on the national economy, since most jobs are generated by SMEs. It should not be forgotten that even in times of an economic boom, companies run into financial difficulties, even bankruptcy. On the one hand, insolvency law can help to keep the damage from insolvency as low as possible for the creditors and to distribute any remaining assets fairly. On the other hand, insolvency law can also help to reorganize the affected company, or a large part of it, out of a (temporary) financial bottleneck and thus to preserve the company and the jobs. International aspects are nowadays present in almost every insolvency, in line with the international interconnections of the affected companies themselves. They might have subsidiaries, branches, office or production sites, employees or simply creditors abroad and this makes the handling of an insolvency – whether for the purpose of liquidation or reorganization – considerably more difficult. If insolvency law does not take these relationships into account and does not offer appropriate and practicable solutions for cross-border situations, then this will often lead to problems in the handling of the insolvency. In the case of liquidation (bankruptcy), this can manifest itself in the fact that individual creditors are given unjustified preference over others. Furthermore, a reorganization may even fail due to a lack of international practicability and thus it might also be possible that the company cannot be rescued.[204]

2. Definitions

2.1 Insolvency

A definition of the term *"insolvency"*, which also represents a worldwide consensus, can be found in the glossary of the UNCITRAL Legislative Guide on Insolvency (UNCITRAL Insolvency Legislative Guide). According to this Legislative Guide, *"insolvency"* exists

> *"when a debtor is generally unable to pay its debts as they mature or when its liabilities exceed the value of its assets."*[205]

The definition of this Legislative Guide contains two facts that lead to insolvency: Insolvency (a company is unable to pay its debts) and overindebtedness (a company's liabilities exceed the value of its assets). The term *"insolvency"* is sometimes also used to refer to the proceedings triggered by an insolvency (in the sense described above). The correct term to use for this purpose is *"insolvency proceedings"*.[206]

2.2. Insolvency proceedings

Once again, the glossary to the UNCITRAL Insolvency Legislative Guide provides a definition of the term *"insolvency proceedings"* that is generally recognized worldwide. According to this definition, insolvency proceedings are

> *"collective proceedings, subject to court supervision, either for reorganization or liquidation."*[207]

---

[204] JOLANTA KREN KOSTIKIEWICZ/RODRIGO RODRIGUEZ, Internationales Insolvenzrecht (2013), p. 3.
[205] Cf. UNCITRAL Legislative Guide on Insolvency (2005), Recommendation 12 (s).
[206] Cf. KREN KOSTIKIEWICZ/RODRIGUEZ, op.cit., pp. 5-6.
[207] Cf. UNCITRAL Legislative Guide on Insolvency (2005),

Despite its shortness, this definition contains the following essential elements:
- it is a matter of *"collective proceedings"*, in contrast to proceedings of individual enforcement (such as the enforcement of seizures or pledges). The principle of collective enforcement always implies that, on the one hand, the entire assets of the debtor are covered and, on the other hand, all creditors (with certain exceptions defined by law) are to be satisfied equally;
- it is a procedure that takes place under *"court supervision"*, i.e., sovereign, judicial supervision, often handled by a state authority itself (in Switzerland frequently the bankruptcy office, occasionally also a bankruptcy administration chosen by the creditors), and
- the proceedings may serve either a reorganization of the debtor (*"reorganization"*) or an orderly liquidation (*"liquidation"* or *"bankruptcy"*).[208]

For example, in Switzerland *"insolvency proceedings"* serves as a generic term for the so-called *"liquidation proceedings"* (*"bankruptcy"*, articles 171 et seq. of the Swiss debt enforcement and bankruptcy law) or as reorganization proceedings (*"moratorium proceedings"*, articles 293 et seq. of the Swiss debt enforcement and bankruptcy law). Accordingly, the term *"insolvency law"* covers both the articles of law dealing with *"bankruptcy proceedings"* (and their effects) and with *"moratorium proceedings"* (and their effects):

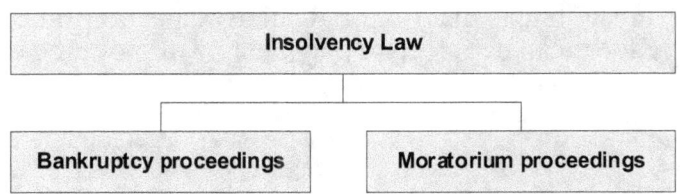

2.3. Bankruptcy proceedings

Bankruptcy (defined here solely as *"bankruptcy proceedings"*) are state-regulated (or at least sovereign-

---

Recommendation 12 (u).
[208] KREN KOSTIKIEWICZ/RODRIGUEZ, op. cit., pp. 6-7.

supervised) compulsory enforcement proceedings for the (basically) equal satisfaction of creditors from the proceeds of the liquidation of the debtor's total assets. This definition contains the following essential elements:
- statutory (not private liquidation);
- state (conducted by a state body, such as the bankruptcy office/court, or a body authorized by it, such as a bankruptcy trustee);
- compulsory (even against the will of the debtor or individual creditors);
- for realization (not for continuation); and
- of all assets for the benefit of all creditors (total execution).

Bankruptcy proceedings are *"insolvency proceedings"* that essentially result in a realization (or liquidation) of the debtor's assets with the primary objective of maximizing the return to creditors.[209]

2.4. Moratorium proceedings

The *"moratorium proceedings"* are a reorganization of a debtor under insolvency law by means of a legally regulated and officially supervised procedure.[210] However, the aim is not the liquidation of the company, but its continuation. This procedure is also ultimately intended to benefit the creditors, since it is based on the idea that the continuation value of the company is higher than the potential liquidation proceeds; the creditors can be forced to play along with this procedure.[211]

---

[209] Cf. KREN KOSTIKIEWICZ/RODRIGUEZ, op. cit., p. 7.
[210] Measures taken outside insolvency proceedings (i.e., before the company is insolvent in the legal sense) on the basis of private law, namely company law like loans, subordination, capital increases, restructuring, etc. are not the subject of this chapter.
[211] LUKAS BOPP, Sanierung im Internationalen Insolvenzverfahren der Schweiz (2004), pp. 7 et seq.

3. International Insolvency Law

3.1. Generally

International insolvency law comprises the legal provisions which deal with insolvency proceedings that have an international connection. A relevant international connection is given if there are relevant connecting factors to more than one state like:
- domicile/registered office of the debtor;
- place of commencement of insolvency proceedings;
- place of a branch office;
- location of assets or parts of the business; and
- domicile/residence of creditors (especially privileged creditors).

International insolvency law can be divided (analogously like private international law) into *international insolvency procedural law* and *international insolvency conflict of laws*.[212]

International Insolvency Law	
International Insolvency Procedural Law	International Insolvency Conflict of Laws
• International jurisdiction • International legal/administrative assistance • Recognition and enforcement of foreign proceedings	• Lex fori concursus • Special connections/links

3.2. International insolvency procedural law

International insolvency procedural law deals with issues that we also know from international private law, i.e.:
- jurisdiction for the opening of insolvency proceedings;
- the recognition of foreign insolvency proceedings and the effects thereof; and in particular
- the recognition or legitimacy of a foreign insolvency administrator/trustee on domestic territory.

The last example makes it clear that international insolvency law is ultimately also a form of international legal assistance (or even international administrative assistance). The effects

---

[212] KREN KOSTIKIEWICZ/RODRIGUEZ, op. cit., pp. 9 et seq.

of a foreign sovereign act (by the insolvency court, insolvency office or other authorities) are extended to the domestic territory (recognition of the insolvency proceedings) and, if applicable, a foreign sovereign person/entity (e.g., insolvency administrator/trustee) is also permitted to carry out its sovereign act in another state.[213]

3.3. International insolvency conflict of laws

International insolvency law can be described as a kind of international conflict of laws in the field of insolvencies in a narrow sense insofar as it deals with the question of the applicable law. International insolvency law is based on the principle that the law of the place where the insolvency proceedings are opened (*lex fori concursus*) applies practically worldwide. However, this principle may be subject to exceptions. Moreover, it applies primarily to matters closely related to the insolvency proceedings.[214]

4. Basic concepts of international insolvency law

4.1 Territoriality vs. universality

4.1.1. Principle of territoriality

The principle of territoriality in insolvency law means that the effects of insolvency proceedings are limited to the territory of the state in which the proceedings are done, and thus only those assets of the debtor located in the state in which the proceedings are conducted are covered.[215]

The decisive factor is that the proceedings are not intended to cover assets located abroad at all (the so-called "*active territoriality principle*"). Consistently implemented, the territoriality principle has the consequence that foreign insolvency proceedings have no influence on the assets of the (foreign) debtor which are located in Switzerland. These

---

[213] KREN KOSTIKIEWICZ/RODRIGUEZ, op. cit., p. 11.
[214] Cf. KREN KOSTIKIEWICZ/RODRIGUEZ, op. cit., pp. 11-12.
[215] Cf. decision of the Swiss Supreme Court 35 I 811.

are withdrawn from the foreign proceedings (so-called *"passive territoriality principle"*). The convergence of the active and passive territoriality principles is the rule, but not without exceptions. Insolvency procedural law governed by the territoriality principle implicitly assumes that in cases where the assets of the debtor are located in different states, separate (territorially valid) proceedings must take place in each state. In this case, the different proceedings are either so-called *"parallel proceedings"* (if each proceeding considers itself as the main proceeding) or one *"main proceeding"* and one or more *"particular proceedings"*.[216]

Court decisions

Subject to other treaty provisions, the effects of an insolvency opened abroad do not extend to the debtor's property and claims located in Switzerland.[217]

Since German law is based on the principle of territoriality and does not recognize Swiss bankruptcy, the pledged objects located in Germany cannot be drawn into the Swiss insolvency estate.[218]

4.1.2. Principle of universality

The principle of universality in insolvency law describes insolvency proceedings which claim to cover all assets of the debtor, irrespective of the national territory in which they are located and also irrespective of whether or not these assets can legally and factually be included in the insolvency estate.[219]

---

[216] ANTON K. SCHNYDER, Insolvenzrecht Deutschlands und der Schweiz – unter Einbezug der EG-Verordnung Nr. 1346/2000, in: Gottwald Peter, Aktuelle Entwicklungen des europäischen und internationalen Zivilverfahrensrechts: ein Forschungsbericht (2002), p. 397 and KREN KOSTIKIEWICZ/RODRIGUEZ, op. cit., pp. 14-15.
[217] Decision of the Swiss Federal Supreme Court 54 III 25.
[218] Cf. Decision of the Swiss Federal Supreme Court 54 III 25.
[219] ALEXANDER TRUNK, Internationales Insolvenzrecht, Systematische Darstellung des deutschen Rechts mit rechtsvergleichenden Bezügen (1998), p. 10.

Court decision

If Swiss law expresses the principle of universality, [...] this is done only in favor of insolvencies opened in Switzerland (...). From the fact that, according to currently undisputed Swiss practice and doctrine, without any treaty linkage, the foreign opening of an insolvency cannot have any attachment effect on assets located in Switzerland, it follows without further ado that assets located on Swiss territory must also remain reserved for the exclusive satisfaction of those creditors who have obtained a valid attachment thereon under Swiss law, and cannot be delivered to a foreign insolvency estate to their detriment.[220]

In consistent implementation of the principle of universality, proceedings opened abroad that claim to have universal validity must also be recognized as such domestically and their effects must be extended to domestic assets (so-called *"passive principle of universality"*). The consistent implementation of the passive universality principle, for example, that insolvency proceedings that have been started abroad have universal validity will also be acknowledged in the inland and its effects encompass also the domestic assets, i.e., there are no domestic insolvency proceedings – at most auxiliary proceedings – and that individual enforcement measures in the debtor's home state (such as an attachment) would be excluded. Therefore, most legal systems (such as the one of Switzerland) only *actively* implement the universality principle, i.e., only with regard to insolvency proceedings started in their own state as main insolvency proceedings). These proceedings often also claim assets located abroad.[221] The principle of universality rarely applies in a *passive* way, at least in autonomous law, but more often in the context of bilateral or multilateral conventions or treaties between the contracting states. Even then, certain proceedings - such as a recognition procedure and/or a domestic auxiliary procedure - are provided for (so-called *"controlled universality"*).[222]

---

[220] Decision of the Swiss Federal Supreme Court 37 Il 587 Consideration 4.
[221] Cf. for example article 197 (1) of the Swiss debt enforcement and bankruptcy law.
[222] KREN KOSTIKIEWICZ/RODRIGUEZ, op. cit., p. 16.

Typical elements of the principle of territory and universality

Principle of territory

- Coverage only of the debtor's assets located in the state where the proceedings were initiated
- Parallel proceedings in states where assets are located
- Satisfaction of domestic creditors only
- Competences of the insolvency administrators are limited to their respective territory
- No recognition of the opening of insolvency proceedings outside the state where the proceedings were initiated
- Possibility of "asset flight"
- Debtor's power to dispose of assets outside the state of commencement not directly affected by the insolvency proceedings
- Foreclosures permitted outside the state where the proceedings were initiated

Principle of universality

- Coverage of all debtor assets regardless of location
- Jurisdiction of a single insolvency authority; no parallel proceedings, at most auxiliary proceedings
- Equal satisfaction of all creditors (no discrimination against foreigners)
- Cross-border competences of insolvency administrators
- Recognition of the opening of insolvency proceedings in all states concerned (ipso iure)
- "Asset flight" is made more difficult
- Debtor's power of disposal over all assets restricted
- Foreclosures not permitted outside the state where the proceedings were initiated

4.1.3. Mediating concepts

The *active universality principle* is the rule. However, very few legal systems – even those that actively apply the universality principle – consistently apply the *passive universality principle*. Mostly, they provide for a recognition procedure with respect to the foreign insolvency decree (with corresponding prerequisites),[223] which, moreover, often entails a territorially limited auxiliary procedure.[224] The doctrine speaks in these cases of "*controlled universality*" or "*mitigated territoriality*". In any case, one can only speak of universality if at least a recognition is provided for in

---

[223] Cf. articles 166 et seq. PILA.
[224] Cf. articles 170 et seq. PILA.

principle and any surplus from an auxiliary bankruptcy is transferred to the foreign estate. Where a legal system in any case conducts particular proceedings within the country and does not *per se* grant any effects to the foreign insolvency claiming universal application, a (at most *"mitigated"*) passive territoriality principle must be assumed.[225]

In summary, it can be said that most states, on the one hand, assume an *active universality principle*, but, on the other hand, make the effects of foreign proceedings on domestically located assets dependent on special conditions and provisions (such as a priority of *"domestic"* creditors as well as certain security interests). Thus, one can at best speak of a controlled passive universality (so for the system of the EU-Regulation 2015/848 on insolvency proceedings of May 20, 2015; also called *"EU Insolvency Regulation"*) or of a *mitigated passive territoriality* (so for the Swiss PILA). The terms are used inconsistently by the doctrine; in the end it depends in each case on the specific implementation. Where the foreign proceedings are not recognized as having any effects, the *active universality principle* is combined with a (pure) *passive territoriality principle*.[226]

4.2 Types of insolvency proceedings

4.2.1. Main insolvency proceedings

The subject of the main insolvency proceedings is the liquidation of all the debtor's assets or the reorganization of the debtor's company as a whole, regardless of the location of these assets. As a rule, the main insolvency proceedings take place at the head office of the company.[227]

> The EU Insolvency Regulation describes the main insolvency proceedings as those *"opened in the member state where the debtor has the center of its main interests"* and which *"have universal scope and are aimed at encompassing all the debtor's assets"*.[228]

---

[225] BOPP, op. cit., p. 86.
[226] KREN KOSTIKIEWICZ/RODRIGUEZ, op. cit., p. 17.
[227] Cf. KREN KOSTIKIEWICZ/RODRIGUEZ, op. cit., p. 19.

As a rule, the main insolvency proceedings are based on the principle of universality.

If main insolvency proceedings are opened in parallel in several states independently of each other (for example, because several states consider the head office of a company to be located in their territory), they are referred to as parallel insolvency proceedings.

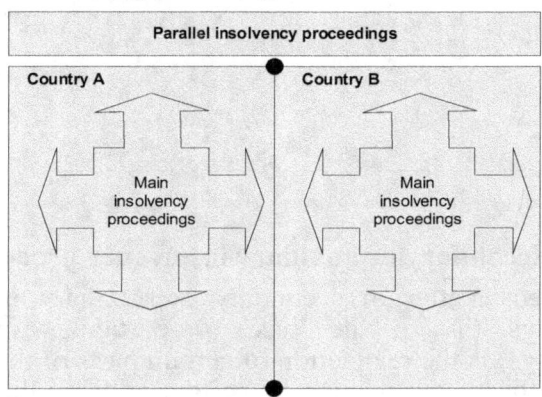

4.2.2. Particular insolvency proceedings

The object of particular insolvency proceedings is the liquidation of certain parts of the debtor's assets or (more rarely) the reorganization of certain parts of the company. In contrast to secondary or auxiliary insolvency proceedings, there is no coordination with any foreign main insolvency proceedings. As a rule, particular insolvency proceedings cover the assets of a company located in the opening state (of the particular insolvency proceedings), which has its head office (and other assets not covered) abroad. A typical starting point for a particular insolvency procedure is a branch office.[229]

---

[228] Cf. consideration 23 of the EU-Regulation 2015/848 on insolvency proceedings of May 20, 2015.
[229] KREN KOSTIKIEWICZ/RODRIGUEZ, op. cit., p. 20.

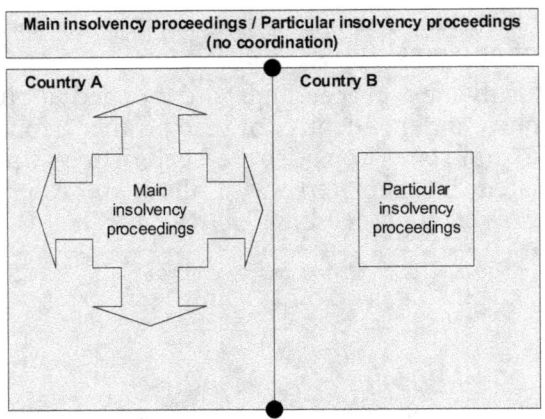

3.2.3. Secondary or auxiliary insolvency proceedings

The subject matter of secondary or auxiliary insolvency proceedings (as in the case of particular insolvency proceedings) is the realization of certain parts of the debtor's assets or the reorganization of certain parts of the debtor's company. As a rule, the particular insolvency proceedings focuses on the assets located in the opening state of such proceedings (and only these).[230]

The EU Insolvency Regulation defines the secondary insolvency proceedings as follows:

"Secondary insolvency proceedings may be opened in the member state where the debtor has an establishment. The effects of secondary insolvency proceedings are limited to the assets located in that state. Mandatory rules of coordination with the main insolvency proceedings satisfy the need for unity in the Union."[231]

However, the main insolvency proceedings concerning the same company in another state are recognized. There is a coordination between the two proceedings and usually any surplus from the secondary insolvency proceedings is going to the main insolvency proceedings. The auxiliary insolvency proceedings provided for in Swiss law under

---

[230] Cf. KREN KOSTIKIEWICZ/RODRIGUEZ, op. cit., pp. 20-21.
[231] Cf. consideration 23 of the EU-Regulation 2015/848 on insolvency proceedings of May 20, 2015.

article 166 PILA are often also referred to as *"PILA bankruptcy procedure"* or *"mini-bankruptcy procedure"*. Such secondary or auxiliary insolvency proceedings are ultimately (due to their territoriality) also particular insolvency proceedings, but a coordination with the main proceedings takes place here; ultimately, they serve the latter. Particular as well as secondary or auxiliary insolvency procedures are based on the principle of territoriality. The latter two, however, also have the purpose of realizing the (active) claim to universality of the foreign main insolvency proceedings as far as possible.[232]

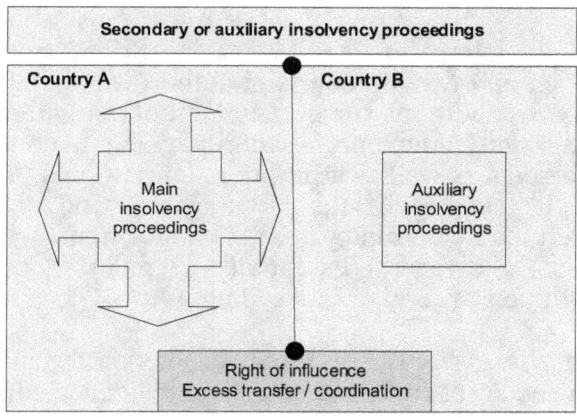

5. Sources of law

5.1 Autonomous Law (Overview)

International insolvency law has a low density of convention/treaty-based regulations. This makes the autonomous, internal insolvency law of each state all the more important. In the following, the autonomous sources of law relevant to Switzerland are briefly described as an example. Of course, with regard to other states, the applicable autonomous international insolvency law of the respective state must be taken into account. In Switzerland, international insolvency law has not undergone any

---

[232] KREN KOSTIKIEWICZ/RODRIGUEZ, op. cit., p. 21.

comprehensive codification. The most relevant legal sources of Swiss insolvency law are the following:[233]

- *Swiss debt enforcement and bankruptcy law*: This act regulates the organization of the debt enforcement and bankruptcy authorities, the debt enforcement and judicial opening proceedings, the (forced) liquidation by way of attachment and foreclosure (individual execution) or by way of bankruptcy (total liquidation) as well as the reorganization agreement. The Swiss debt enforcement and bankruptcy law is supplemented by various ordinances.

- *PILA*: In international relations, the PILA regulates the jurisdiction of Swiss courts or authorities, the applicable law, the conditions for the recognition and enforcement of foreign judgments, bankruptcy and composition agreements as well as arbitration. Of particular interest is the 11th chapter of the law (articles 166-175 PILA) concerning bankruptcy and composition agreements (which, however, essentially regulates only the recognition of foreign proceedings).[234]

- *Special provisions*: Special provisions on the insolvency of financial institutions (banks and insurance companies) are common in most jurisdictions as it is in Switzerland.

5.2 Convention/Treaties and European Secondary Legislation

5.2.1. Istanbul Convention

The Council of Europe drafted an *"European Convention on Certain Aspects of International Bankruptcy"* of June 5, 1990, which is also called *"Istanbul Convention"* and provides for the following main regulatory content:[235]

---

[233] KREN KOSTIKIEWICZ/RODRIGUEZ, op. cit., pp. 27-28.
[234] RICHARD GASSMANN/FLORIAN BOMMER, Handbuch Internationales Handels- und Wirtschaftsrecht, Rechtliche Herausforderungen im Auslandsgeschäft (2015), pp. 710-711.
[235] KREN KOSTIKIEWICZ/RODRIGUEZ, op. cit., pp. 28-29.

- It enables the bankruptcy trustee appointed in the state where the bankruptcy was opened to directly exercise certain powers (administration and supervision of the debtor's assets and disposition thereof) in the states where the bankrupt's assets are located, whereby the trustee must comply with the national law of the state in which he intends to operate.
- It enables the opening of auxiliary or secondary bankruptcies. A secondary bankruptcy may be opened in any other contracting state in which the bankrupt has assets, without it being necessary to establish his insolvency locally; the mere reference to the main bankruptcy already opened is sufficient. It is always presupposed that the main bankruptcy venue complies with the provisions on indirect jurisdiction.
- In cases where creditors are spread over the territory of several contracting parties, the Istanbul Convention allows these creditors to lodge their claims in the bankruptcy opened in another state simply and with few formalities.

The required number of ratifications (3) for entry into force have never been achieved due to 79 political differences. With the entry into force of the European Insolvency Regulation, the Istanbul Convention has definitely become obsolete.

5.2.2. EU Insolvency Regulation

The EU Regulation 2015/848 on insolvency proceedings of May 20, 2015 ("*EU Insolvency Regulation*") regulates the (international) jurisdiction to open insolvency proceedings and judgments directly related to such proceedings, as well as the recognition of the effects of such proceedings and judgments and the powers of insolvency practitioners in their cross-border activities. In addition, the EU Insolvency Regulation contains provisions on the law applicable to insolvency proceedings and related matters. It is in force for all EU member states except Denmark.

The EU Insolvency Regulation thus contains a very comprehensive regulation of international insolvency law. In terms of content, it is based in part on the (failed) Istanbul

Convention of 1990. It is still left to the member states to determine the form of insolvency proceedings (which thus continue to differ from state to state), including any secondary or auxiliary insolvency proceedings.

5.2.3. Bilateral Agreements

The existing bilateral agreements between the EU member states in the field of insolvency law have largely been rendered meaningless by the EU Insolvency Regulation.

For example, the Nordic Bankruptcy Convention of November 7, 1933, which has been ratified by Denmark, Finland, Iceland, Norway and Sweden, is now only relevant for the relationship between Norway and the other contracting states and in the relationship between Denmark (to which the EU Insolvency Regulation does not apply) and the other contracting states.

Outside Europe, the Código Bustamante of February 20, 1928, which applies to numerous South American states, has to be mentioned.

5.3 Non-binding multinational regulations

5.3.1. UNCITRAL Model Law on Cross-Border Insolvency

UNCITRAL stands for *"United Nations Commission on International Trade Law"*, a United Nations commission specializing in trade law issues with headquarters in Vienna and New York. UNCITRAL has issued numerous sets of rules in the form of conventions, model laws or recommendations on various areas of commercial law (in a broad sense), such as the Vienna Sales Convention (CISG) or the UNCITRAL Arbitration Rules. The UNCITRAL Model Law on Cross-Border Insolvency of December 15, 1997 (*"UNCITRAL Insolvency Model Law"*) contains provisions on access of foreign insolvency administrators to the courts of another state, on cooperation between insolvency administrators and courts of different states, and on recognition of foreign insolvency proceedings. As a model law, it contains normative provisions that are not binding *per se*, but are recommended for adoption into national law.[236] In particular, the US international insolvency law (Chapter 13 of the US Bankruptcy Code) is taken almost *verbatim* from the UNCITRAL Insolvency Model Law.

5.3.2. UNCITRAL Legislative Guide on Insolvency Law

The Legislative Guide on Insolvency Law from 2004 (*"UNCITRAL Insolvency Legislative Guide"*), which was also prepared within the framework of UNCITRAL, contains recommendations on the structure of (internal, autonomous) insolvency law. In terms of form and content, it ultimately represents a guide for the legislator to enact effective, comprehensive and up-to-date insolvency law. A *"legislative guide"* is probably the most open and non-binding form of international standardization (probably the *"softest soft law"* imaginable). In terms of form and content, it is aimed in particular at developing and emerging countries which have had no or only very rudimentary regulations on insolvency law. At the same time, it represents an extremely well-founded scholarly work, in which ultimately the formulation of common legal figures and a *"worldwide consensus"* on the formulation of insolvency law emerge. Accordingly, the definitions contained in the legislative guide are particularly valuable. The recommendations in the accompanying commentary also contain a valuable catalog and, in some cases, an explanation of legal figures from practically all legal regimes of the world. Valuable suggestions for the further development of older *"set"* legal systems, such as Switzerland's, can also be found therein. Particularly in international insolvency law, the legislative guide – comparable to the UNIDROIT Principles in private law – has an important function as a common point of reference for the interpretation of concepts and legal figures.[237]

---

[236] KREN KOSTIKIEWICZ/RODRIGUEZ, op. cit., p. 31.
[237] Cf. KREN KOSTIKIEWICZ/RODRIGUEZ, op. cit., p. 32.

6. Unified International Insolvency Law: EU Insolvency Regulation and UNCITRAL Insolvency Model Law

6.1. EU Insolvency Regulation

6.1.1. Background and Objectives

On May 29, 2000, the Council of the EU adopted the Regulation on insolvency proceedings. It entered into force on May 31, 2002. Thanks to this regulation, for the first time there is a uniform regulation of international insolvency law in the European Union (excluding Denmark). The Regulation was preceded by numerous unsuccessful negotiations on a possible international convention (e.g., the aforementioned Istanbul Convention of June 5, 1990). The new version of the EU Insolvency Regulation adopted by the European Parliament and the Council on May 20, 2015 entered into force on June 26, 2017, replacing the previous version. It is applicable to all cross-border insolvency proceedings in the EU opened after that date.

The objective of the EU Insolvency Regulation is the EU-wide enforcement of the principle of universality, i.e., the recognition of the foreign effects of insolvency proceedings, albeit in a sense modified by (national, territorial) secondary insolvency proceedings (*"modified"* or *"controlled"* universality). The regulation is characterized by the fact that it basically starts from a universal procedure recognized by all EU member states (main insolvency proceedings), which has a claim of validity with respect to all debtor assets located in the member states. However, it also grants the possibility of secondary insolvency proceedings, which can be opened in the respective EU member states.[238]

6.1.2. Scope of application

The EU Insolvency Regulation only covers cross-border insolvency proceedings within the EU internal market (with the exception of Denmark). Thus, the debtor must have the

---

[238] KREN KOSTIKIEWICZ/RODRIGUEZ, op. cit., p. 169.

center of its main interests ("*center of main interest*" (CoMI)) in a member state subject to the EU Insolvency Regulation. If such center of main interest is located in a third country (e.g., Switzerland), it does not apply. If the debtor operates a branch outside the internal market, but the center of main interest is located in another member state, the EU Insolvency Regulation nevertheless remains applicable. The material scope of application of the EU Insolvency Regulation includes all overall proceedings which presuppose the insolvency of the debtor and result in the total or partial seizure of assets of the debtor and the appointment of an administrator (article 1 EU Insolvency Regulation). The EU Insolvency Regulation itself does not determine when an insolvency exists, but leaves this to the respective law of the member states; Annex A of the EU Insolvency Regulation lists the procedures of the respective countries. In principle, natural persons and legal entities such as companies fall within its scope. This Regulation does not apply to proceedings in respect of insurance undertakings, credit institutions, investment firms and undertakings for collective investment. The EU Insolvency Regulation sets also the framework for international group insolvency or group insolvency proceedings. In addition to provisions for cooperation and coordination of parties in pending insolvency proceedings of several group companies, group coordination proceedings are now also possible, provided that the law of the member state provides for such proceedings.[239]

---

[239] KREN KOSTIKIEWICZ/RODRIGUEZ, op. cit., pp. 170-171.

Scope of application		
Territorial scope of application	**Material scope of application**	**Applicability in time**
• International matters • Center of the debtor's main interests is in the EU area (exception Denmark)	• Insolvency proceedings (see Article 2 (4) EU Insolvency Regulation and list in Annex A with all proceedings in each country). • This Regulation shall not apply to proceedings that concern (see article 1 (2) EU Insolvency Regulation): (i) insurance undertakings (ii) credit institutions (iii) investment firms and other firms, institutions and undertakings to the extent that they are covered by Directive 2001/24/EC (iv) collective investment undertakings	• The provisions of this Regulation shall apply only to insolvency proceedings opened after June 26, 2017. • Acts committed by a debtor before that date shall continue to be governed by the law which was applicable to them at the time when they were committed (article 84 (1) EU Insolvency Regulation)

6.1.3. Jurisdiction for main and secondary insolvency proceedings

The main concern of the EU Insolvency Regulation is that main insolvency proceedings opened in a member state should cover all the debtor's assets located throughout the EU in accordance with the principle of universality. To this end, it must be ensured that only one main insolvency proceeding is opened throughout the EU. Article 3 (1)

Sentence 1 EU Insolvency Regulation directly sets out the international jurisdiction for the opening of main insolvency proceedings: *"The courts of the member state within the territory of which the center of the debtor's main interests is situated shall have jurisdiction to open insolvency proceedings ('main insolvency proceedings'). The center of main interests shall be the place where the debtor conducts the administration of its interests on a regular basis and which is ascertainable by third parties."*

In the case of a company or legal person, the place of the registered office shall be presumed to be the CoMI in the absence of proof to the contrary (article 3 (1) sentence 2 EU Insolvency Regulation, incorporation principle as the starting point). The statutory seat thus establishes a (rebuttable) presumption in favor of the center of its main interests at this location. The party claiming that the CoMI is not located at the statutory seat must therefore provide evidence to the contrary and show that the CoMI is rather located in another state.

However, case law attaches great weight to the legal presumption in favor of the statutory seat: According to the much-respected Eurofoods-decision of the ECJ, this presumption can only be rebutted if it is proven that the debtor carries out its main activity in another country and that it does not carry out any activity at the location of the statutory seat. In a more recent decision (Interedil), the ECJ has clarified its case law.

Interedil Srl v. Fallimento Interedil Srl and Intesa Gestione Crediti SpA
(C-396/09)

Facts

Interedil was an Italian incorporated and registered company. In July 2001 Interedil was registered in England and removed from the Italian companies' registry. It is apparent from the ECJ's judgment that the registration as a foreign company (with a UK establishment) and removal from the Italian companies' registry was viewed as amounting to a transfer of Interedil's registered office from Italy to the UK. At around the same time as Interedil was registered as a foreign company in England, its business was acquired by a British group of companies and title to Interedil's assets was subsequently transferred to an English registered company. Interedil was removed from the UK foreign companies' registry in July 2002 (meaning that Interedil was not registered at all in any companies' registry) and, in October 2003, an application for the opening of bankruptcy proceedings in respect of Interedil was made to the Italian court. Interedil argued that the Italian court had no jurisdiction to commence insolvency proceedings as following the transfer of its registered office to the UK, only the UK courts had jurisdiction to commence such proceedings. As a result, questions concerning, *inter alia*, the meaning of the CoMI (in particular the strength of the registered office presumption) and establishment were referred to the ECJ by the Italian Supreme Court, albeit with the reference made on the assumption that the company's most recent registered office was in England.

Decision

Having considered the ECJ's judgments in Eurofood and in Staubitz-Schreiber, the ECJ held as follows:

Centre of main interests: CoMI must be interpreted in a uniform way by EU member states and by reference to EU law and not national laws.

(i) If a debtor's registered office is moved before a request to open insolvency proceedings is made, the debtor's CoMI is presumed to be the place of its new registered office. As Interedil had ceased to be registered anywhere and had ceased all activities a few months before the application to open insolvency proceedings was made, the question for the ECJ was how a corporate debtor's CoMI is to be assessed when the debtor has no registered office or activities by the time the application to open insolvency proceedings is made. In these circumstances, the ECJ held that CoMI is established by looking at the last location of the debtor's registered office (which appears to have been presumed to be in England) and the factors that existed at that time (i.e., at the time the debtor was removed from all companies' registries; where it was last registered and the activities that existed at that time). The court so ruled on the footing that this location would be the place which, from an objective viewpoint and one ascertainable by third parties, the company had the closest links.

(ii) A debtor's CoMI must be determined by attaching greater importance to the place of the company's central administration, as may be established by objective factors which are ascertainable by third parties. Where a company's registered office and place of central administration are in the same jurisdiction, the registered office presumption cannot be rebutted. Where a company's central administration is not in the same place as its registered office, the presence of assets belonging to the debtor and the existence of contracts for financial exploitation of those assets in an EU member state, other than that in which the registered office is situated, are not sufficient factors to rebut the registered office presumption, unless a comprehensive assessment of all the relevant factors makes it possible to establish, in a manner that is ascertainable by third parties, that the company's central administration is located in that other EU member state.

(iii) Factors to be taken into account when analyzing whether the registered office presumption has been rebutted include, in particular, all places in which the debtor company pursues economic activities and all those in which it holds assets, insofar as those places are ascertainable by third parties. Such factors must be assessed in a comprehensive manner, taking into account the individual circumstances of each particular case.

(iv) The requirement that the factors used to rebut the registered office presumption must be objectively ascertainable by third parties may be considered to be met where the material factors have been made public, or at the very least, made sufficiently accessible to enable third parties, in particular the company's creditors, to be aware of them.

In addition to the main insolvency proceedings, the EU Insolvency Regulation permits further, territorially limited insolvency proceedings, the *particular insolvency proceedings*, which can be opened in the state of an establishment *before* the main insolvency proceedings (article 3 (4) EU Insolvency Regulation) and the *secondary insolvency proceedings*, which can be opened at the place of an establishment of the debtor *after* the main insolvency proceedings (article 3 (3) EU Insolvency Regulation). Secondary insolvency proceedings are opened without a new examination of the insolvency. The purpose of the secondary insolvency proceedings is to facilitate the liquidation of the foreign assets for the insolvency administrator of the main insolvency proceedings. This is achieved, for example, by legally anchored duties of cooperation and information between the various administrators. At the same time, however, the territorial insolvency proceedings (as particular or secondary insolvency proceedings) supersede the effects of the main proceedings in the state concerned. *Particular insolvency proceedings* opened *before* the opening of the main proceedings become *ipso iure secondary insolvency proceedings* with the opening of the main proceedings abroad (and their automatic recognition in a member state).[240]

---

[240] KREN KOSTIKIEWICZ/RODRIGUEZ, op. cit., pp. 172-173.

International jurisdiction		
Main insolvency proceedings	**Special insolvency proceedings**	
Member state within the territory of which the CoMI is situated (presumption) • *Company or legal person:* the place of the registered office = CoMI • *Individual excercising business or professional activity:* principal place of business = CoMI (presumption) • *Any other individual:* individual's habitual residence = CoMI	**Secondary insolvency proceedings** Where main insolvency proceedings have been opened, any proceedings opened subsequently are secondary insolvency proceedings.	**Particular insolvency proceedings** Where main insolvency proceedings have been opened, any proceedings opened priorly are particular insolvency proceedings.
	Jurisdiction	
	Member state in which the debtor has an establishment	
Principle of universality Extension of effect to all member states. Realization of all assets of the debtor with participation of all creditors.	**Principle of territoriality**	
	Effect of proceedings limited to opening state	
	Realization of the debtor's assets located in the respective state	
	Cooperation with the main insolvency proceedings	Independent insolvency proceedings

6.1.4. Effects of recognition and secondary proceedings

The EU Insolvency Regulation is based on the principle of automatic recognition. The opening of insolvency proceedings by the court with international jurisdiction is recognized *ipso iure* in all other member states without formalities (such as exequatur proceedings; article 19 EU Insolvency Regulation). A prerequisite for the recognition of insolvency proceedings concerning the assets of a debtor is that the court decision to start the proceedings has been opened in the state competent according to article 3 EU Insolvency Regulation. The decision must be effective, but not (yet) necessarily legally valid. The recognition obligation provides for exceptions (within very narrow limits). For example, the courts of another member state may refuse recognition or enforcement if the decision is incompatible with the public policy of that state (article 33 EU Insolvency Regulation). However, such cases are rare. The primary consequence of the extension of effect is that the liquidator in the main insolvency proceedings may exercise all the powers to which he is entitled in the opening state (with the exception of coercive measures) and in the other member states as well, in particular he may take assets located there (not encumbered with security interests, see articles 8 and 10 EU Insolvency Regulation) to the estate (article 21 EU Insolvency Regulation). The recognition also has the following effects (examples):[241]

- The foreign administrator of the main proceedings is entitled to apply for the realization of a property or an entry in the land register in another member state;
- The domestic creditor must – in the case of recognition of a composition agreement – in principle accept the claim-limiting effect of a settlement concluded in foreign proceedings.

However, the automatic extension of effects (universality) is modified by any secondary insolvency proceedings opened (or converted from original particular proceedings into such) (principle of modified universality). The secondary insolvency proceedings prevent the main proceedings from having any effect on the assets in the state of the secondary proceedings. The administrators of both proceedings are obliged to cooperate and exchange information (article 41 EU Insolvency Regulation). Each administrator may enter the claims of *"his"* creditors in the other proceedings. The administrator of the main proceedings may, for example, request the suspension of the liquidation in the secondary proceedings (article 46 EU Insolvency Regulation). Probate agreements are only possible upon proposal and with the consent of the main insolvency administrator (article 47 EU Insolvency Regulation). Secondary insolvency proceedings

---

[241] KREN KOSTIKIEWICZ/RODRIGUEZ, op. cit., p. 177.

under the EU Insolvency Regulation require the existence of an establishment (cf. its definition in article 2 (10) EU Insolvency Regulation) of the debtor in the relevant state. The simple location of assets is not sufficient.[242]

> **Interedil Srl v. Fallimento Interedil Srl and Intese Gestione Crediti SpA, European Court of Justice (C-396/09)**
>
> The term *"establishment"* within the meaning of the EU Insolvency Regulation must be interpreted as requiring the presence/existence aimed at carrying on an economic activity, with a minimum degree of organization and a certain degree of stability. The mere existence of individual assets or bank accounts does not, in principle, meet the definition. An establishment must be determined in the same manner as CoMI - i.e., on the basis of objective factors which are ascertainable by third parties.

Any surplus from the secondary proceedings shall be transferred to the main proceedings (article 49 EU Insolvency Regulation). The extension of the effects of the main proceedings is further limited by exceptions to the principle of *lex fori concursus*, which leads to the application of foreign law to certain legal effects (and, if applicable, a limitation of the effects of the main proceedings).[243]

6.1.5. Recognition of judgments related to insolvency

In addition to the opening of proceedings (and the legal consequences directly connected therewith), recognition or extension of effects also includes, on the basis of article 32 EU Insolvency Regulation:
– the other decisions of the insolvency court issued for the conduct and termination of insolvency proceedings,
– decisions made directly as a result of the insolvency proceedings and closely connected therewith, and
– Decisions on protective measures in the opening proceedings.[244]

---

[242] KREN KOSTIKIEWICZ/RODRIGUEZ, op. cit., p. 178.
[243] Cf. KREN KOSTIKIEWICZ/RODRIGUEZ, op. cit., p. 178.

Recognition of foreign insolvency proceedings	
General Rule: Recognition *ipso iure* (article 19 (1) EU Insolvency Regulation), if • Insolvency proceeding according to the EU Insolvency Regulation • Insolvency proceeding has been opened by a court • No infringement of the public policy order	
Effects of recognition	
Main insolvency proceedings	Secondary insolvency proceedings
The judgment opening insolvency shall, with no further formalities, produce the same effects in any other member state (article 20 (1) EU Insolvency Regulation) *Powers of the insolvency practitioner:* (i) may exercise all the powers conferred to it, by the law of the state of the opening of proceedings, in another member state (article 21 (1) EU Insolvency Regulation), and (ii) in exercising its powers, the insolvency practitioner shall comply with the law of the member state within the territory of which it intends to take action, in particular with regard to procedures for the realization of assets. Those powers may not include coercive measures, unless ordered by a court of that member state, or the right to rule on legal proceedings or disputes (article 21 (1) EU Insolvency Regulation)	The effects of the proceedings may not be challenged in other member states. Any restriction of creditors' rights, in particular a stay or discharge, shall produce effects vis-à-vis assets situated within the territory of another member state only in the case of those creditors who have given their consent (article 20 (2) EU Insolvency Regulation) *Powers of the insolvency practitioner:* The insolvency practitioner appointed by a court may in any other member state claim through the courts or out of court that moveable property was removed from the territory of the state of the opening of proceedings to the territory of that other member state after the opening of the insolvency proceedings. The insolvency practitioner may also bring any action to set aside which is in the interests of the creditors (article 21 (2) EU Insolvency Regulation)
Limitation: Practitioner has these powers only as long as no other insolvency proceedings have been opened there and no preservation measure to the contrary has been taken there further to a request for the opening of insolvency proceedings in that state (article 20 (3) EU Insolvency Regulation).	
Recognition and enforcement of other judgement:	
Recognition: Judgments handed down by a court whose judgment concerning the opening of proceedings is recognized and which concern the course and closure of insolvency proceedings, and compositions approved by that court, shall also be recognized with no further formalities (article 32 (1) EU Insolvency Regulation) *Enforcement*: Such judgments shall be enforced in a formal exequatur proceeding (article 32 (2) EU Insolvency Regulation) *Limitation*: No infringement of the public policy order	

6.1.6. Applicable Law

As a basic rule, article 7 EU Insolvency Regulation assumes the validity of the *lex fori concursus*. The law of the place where the insolvency proceedings are opened therefore governs, for example, the conditions under which the proceedings are opened, how they are to be conducted and

---

[244] KREN KOSTIKIEWICZ/RODRIGUEZ, op. cit., pp. 178-179.

terminated, and the substantive private law effects of the opening of the proceedings.

7. UNCITRAL Model Law on Cross-border Insolvency

7.1. Background and subject matter

In 1997, the UNCITRAL Working Group on Insolvency Law completed its work on the Model Law on Cross-Border Insolvency, which was adopted by the UNCITRAL General Assembly in May of the same year. The content of the Model Law was significantly influenced by the EU Convention on Insolvency Proceedings of November 25, 1995 (which never entered into force as such, but did so slightly altered in the form of the EU Insolvency Regulation). The Model Law regulates the conditions under which the administrator of foreign insolvency proceedings is granted access to the courts of a state which has also adopted the Model Law, the conditions under which foreign insolvency proceedings are recognized and protective measures can be ordered in favor of the foreign administrator, how courts and insolvency administrators in different countries can cooperate more efficiently and how several insolvency proceedings commenced simultaneously in different countries are coordinated. The Model Law, on the other hand, does not contain any provisions on applicable law, nor does it contain any provisions on direct jurisdiction. To assist countries in drafting insolvency law based on the Model Law, a *"Guide to Enactment of the UNCITRAL Model Law on Cross-border Insolvency"* has been published. This is directed primarily to executive branches of governments and legislators preparing the necessary enacting legislation, but it also provides useful insight for those charged with interpretation and application of the Model Law, such as judges, and other users of the text, such as practitioners and academics. As mentioned above, the text of the law was enacted in the form of a Model Law. This means of international legal harmonization goes less far than a convention (no direct binding effect and no need for signature or ratification). A model law is intended to serve as a template for countries that intend to enact a law in the regulated area (or to adapt the existing one).[245] In the meantime, legislation based on the Model Law has been adopted in a total of 58 states. Important countries such as Japan (2000), the USA (2005), or Great Britain (2006) have incorporated the Model Law more or less *verbatim* into their national law, others have at least been inspired by it.[246]

7.2. Main Features of the UNCITRAL Model Law

7.2.1. Generally

The Model Law basically covers the international aspects of insolvency law. The structure of the Model Law is essentially based on three pillars: one pillar is the recognition of foreign insolvency proceedings within the country. In addition, access of foreign bankruptcy trustees and creditors to domestic courts, to other authorities and to domestic bankruptcy proceedings is made possible, and cross-border cooperation between bankruptcy trustees and courts is facilitated and promoted. The applicable law is not subject of the UNCITRAL Insolvency Model Law. To circumscribe the substantive scope of application and to promote a uniform application of the UNCITRAL Insolvency Model Law contains a list of definitions of terms. The Model Law excludes certain institutions or entities such as banks or insurance companies from its scope of application. These are usually subject to specific legislation in the states.[247]

UNCITRAL MODEL LAW ON INSOLVENCY

Chapter I. General provisions

---

[245] KREN KOSTIKIEWICZ/RODRIGUEZ, op. cit., p. 187.
[246] Cf. world-wide status of the enactment of the UNCITRAL Model Law: https://uncitral.un.org/en/texts/insolvency/modellaw/cross-border_insolvency/status.
[247] KREN KOSTIKIEWICZ/RODRIGUEZ, op. cit., p. 186.

Article 1. Scope of application

Article 2. Definitions

Article 3. International obligations of this State

Article 4. [Competent court or authority]

Article 5. Authorization of [insert the title of the person or body administering a reorganization or liquidation under the law of the enacting State] to act in a foreign State

Article 6. Public policy exception

Article 7. Additional assistance under other laws

Article 8. Interpretation

United States: Iida v Kitahara (In re Iida) 377 B.R. 243, 259 (B.A.P. 9th Cir. 2007)

Three principles have been identified in the case law of one state to guide courts in analyzing whether an action taken in a recognition proceeding is manifestly contrary to the public policy of that State under the equivalent of article 6 of the UNCITRAL MODEL LAW

(a) The mere fact of a conflict between foreign law and local law, absent other considerations, is insufficient to support the invocation of the public policy exception;

(b) Deference to a foreign proceeding should not be afforded in a recognition proceeding where the procedural fairness of the foreign proceeding is in doubt or cannot be cured by the adoption of additional protections;

(c) An action should not be taken in a recognition proceeding where taking that action would frustrate the ability of the courts to administer the recognition proceeding and/or impinge severely on a local constitutional or statutory right, particularly if a party continues to enjoy the benefits of the recognition proceeding.

7.2.2. Access of foreign bankruptcy trustees and creditors

Chapter II regulates the rights of foreign liquidators and creditors in domestic insolvency proceedings. In principle, the foreign bankruptcy trustee should be able to open or participate in domestic insolvency proceedings without his legitimacy being called into question, in particular without first having to go through a recognition procedure. Furthermore, Chapter II contains the important principle of non-discrimination against foreign creditors in entering claims and triggering insolvency proceedings.[248]

> **UNCITRAL MODEL LAW ON INSOLVENCY**
>
> *Chapter II. Access of foreign representatives and creditors to courts in this state*
>
> Article 9. Right of direct access
>
> Article 10. Limited jurisdiction
>
> Article 11. Application by a foreign representative to commence a proceeding under [identify laws of the enacting State relating to insolvency]
>
> Article 12. Participation of a foreign representative in a proceeding under [identify laws of the enacting State relating to insolvency]
>
> Article 13. Access of foreign creditors to a proceeding under [identify laws of the enacting State relating to insolvency]
>
> Article 14. Notification to foreign creditors of a proceeding under [identify laws of the enacting State relating to insolvency]

---

[248] KREN KOSTIKIEWICZ/RODRIGUEZ, op. cit., p. 187.

7.2.3. Recognition of foreign insolvency proceedings

The extension of the effect of foreign insolvency proceedings to the domestic market requires (like the Swiss model) a recognition procedure. During the recognition proceedings, the court may, upon request, already order precautionary measures for the protection of creditors. Only foreign main insolvency proceedings are open for recognition. Foreign proceedings qualify as main insolvency proceedings if they have been instituted at the debtor's registered office, i.e., at the CoMI. On the other hand, it is referred to as secondary insolvency proceedings if the debtor only has an establishment in the opening state. Recognition of the foreign main proceedings may, but need not, be followed by territorially limited secondary insolvency proceedings, provided there is an establishment in the state concerned. The proceedings in question must be a *"foreign insolvency proceeding"* within the meaning of the UNCITRAL Insolvency Model Law, i.e., a proceeding of total enforcement under sovereign, judicial or administrative supervision, with the assets of the debtor under the supervision of the latter, with the aim of carrying out a reorganization or liquidation. The UNCITRAL Insolvency Model Law provides for the general reservation of recognition of the public policy violation. On the other hand, recognition may not be made conditional on reciprocity. Article 20 of the UNCITRAL Insolvency Model Law provides for the following effects in the case of recognition of main proceedings, which automatically come into force with the valid recognition or are issued by the competent court:

- Individual proceedings concerning the debtor's assets are suspended,
- seizures of the debtor's assets are suspended, and
- the debtor loses the freedom to dispose of his assets.

Further effects can be applied for with the recognition or at a later date. However, the effects in the state of recognition are significantly limited if secondary insolvency proceedings are opened there (at the request of the foreign insolvency administrator or a creditor).[249]

---

[249] KREN KOSTIKIEWICZ/RODRIGUEZ, op. cit., pp. 188-189.

UNCITRAL MODEL LAW ON INSOLVENCY

Chapter III. Recognition of a foreign proceeding and relief

Article 15. Application for recognition of a foreign proceeding

Article 16. Presumptions concerning recognition

Article 17. Decision to recognize a foreign proceeding

Article 18. Subsequent information

Article 19. Relief that may be granted upon application for recognition of foreign proceeding

Article 20. Effects of recognition of a foreign main proceeding

Article 21. Relief that may be granted upon recognition of a foreign proceeding

Article 22. Protection of creditors and other interested persons

Article 23. Actions to avoid acts detrimental to creditors

Article 24. Intervention by a foreign representative in proceedings in this State

Recognition and Enforcement Effects under the UNCITRAL Model Law - Overview

Application by the foreign insolvency administration for recognition of the foreign insolvency proceedings

- Jurisdiction: Place of the court designated in article 4 of the UNCITRAL Model Law.
- Possibility to issue protective measures (article 19 UNCITRAL Model Law)
- Conditions for recognition (formal procedure; article 17 UNCITRAL Model Law)
- Foreign insolvency proceedings within the meaning of Article 2 (b) UNCITRAL Model Law
- Applicant is a person or institution within the meaning of article 2 (b) UNCITRAL Model Law
- Submission of certain documents (article 15 UNCITRAL Model Law)
- Application has been submitted to the court designated in article 4 UNCITRAL Model Law.
- Jurisdiction of the foreign insolvency proceedings:
    (i) Foreign main proceeding according to article 2 (b) UNCITRAL Model Law: place of the CoMI of the debtor in the opening state.
    (ii) Particular proceedings ("foreign non main proceeding"; article 2 (c) UNCITRAL Model Law: establishment according to article 2 (f) UNCITRAL Model Law) of the debtor in the opening state (article 17 (2) (b) UNCITRAL Model Law)

Recognition of the foreign bankruptcy decree		
Automatic consequences: The foreign insolvency administrator obtains the right to directly access the court and thus legal protection in the recognizing state. He can participate in any secondary proceedings that may take place there (article 12 UNCITRAL Model Law). Initiate avoidance proceedings (article 23 UNCITRAL Model Law) or intervene in pending proceedings (article 27 UNCITRAL Model Law).		
Main proceedings • The individual proceedings against the debtor are discontinued ("stay"; article 20 (1) (a) and (b) UNCITRAL Model Law; • The debtor loses its power of disposal ("freeze"; article 20 (1) (c) UNCITRAL Model Law)		**Particular proceedings**
Further consequences: All further consequences of recognition are at the discretion of the recognizing state. Article 21 UNCITRAL Model Law contains an exemplary list of legal consequences that are pronounced at the request of the foreign bankruptcy administration. With respect to the realization of the domestic assets, the following options are open to the recognizing state:		
Transfer of the domestic assets to the main bankruptcy estate Transfer of the administration, realization and distribution of the domestic assets to the foreign administrator; provided that the interests of the domestic creditors in the foreign proceedings are safeguarded (article 21 (2) UNCITRAL Model Law).		**Conduct of secondary proceedings** Administration, realization and distribution of the domestic assets by means of secondary proceedings (article 20 (4), article 28 UNCITRAL Model Law). See Chapter IV regarding Cooperation with foreign courts and foreign representatives (article 25-27 UNCITRAL Model Law) and Chapter V regarding concurrent proceedings (articles 28-32 UNCITRAL Model Law).

7.2.4. Cross-border cooperation

One focus of the UNCITRAL Insolvency Model Law is on cooperation between the courts and the various competent authorities. In many national insolvency legislations, international cooperation is not mentioned or its scope is uncertain. The UNCITRAL Insolvency Model Law fills this gap and explicitly authorizes courts and authorities to engage in such cooperation. For example, it provides for the transmission of information, the coordination of the administration and supervision of the debtor's assets and business, and the court approval or implementation of agreements to coordinate concurrently pending insolvency proceedings. The provisions of the UNCITRAL Insolvency Model Law on cooperation are also intended to encourage courts and insolvency administrators to make use of the possibility to conclude so-called *"insolvency protocols"*. These are agreements between insolvency courts of different countries or between insolvency administrators (or administrators and courts) on the modalities of cooperation and exchange of information. Such *"protocols"* are widespread in Anglo-American legal circles, and are increasingly finding their way into civil-law legal practice. They can regulate the modalities of communication (e.g., to whom which notifications are to be sent), but also delimit responsibilities (e.g., over certain assets) and allocate costs.[250]

UNCITRAL MODEL LAW ON INSOLVENCY

Chapter IV. Cooperation with foreign courts and foreign representatives

Article 25. Cooperation and direct communication between a court of this state and foreign courts or foreign representatives

Article 26. Cooperation and direct communication between the [insert the title of a person or body administering a reorganization or liquidation under the law of the enacting state] and foreign courts or foreign representatives

Article 27. Forms of cooperation

7.2.5. Coordination of parallel insolvency proceedings

The provisions of article 28 et seq. UNCITRAL Insolvency Model Law refer, on the one hand, to proceedings that are opened after the recognition of the foreign main insolvency proceedings. Here, the Model Law allows such secondary

---

[250] KREN KOSTIKIEWICZ/RODRIGUEZ, op. cit., p. 191

insolvency proceedings, provided they are limited to the assets in the opening state and coordination with the main insolvency proceedings is ensured (i.e., they are structured as auxiliary proceedings). Alternatively, they also anticipate the inherently pathological case of parallel insolvency proceedings in different states. Foreign parallel insolvency proceedings should also be able to have certain effects (subject to the domestic proceedings), and in any case the individual insolvency proceedings should be coordinated. Furthermore, article 32 states that a creditor in the domestic insolvency proceedings must take into account the proceeds of the foreign insolvency proceedings, a principle which is also familiar to Swiss law.[251]

UNCITRAL MODEL LAW ON INSOLVENCY

Chapter V. Concurrent proceedings

Article 28. Commencement of a proceeding under [identify laws of the enacting State relating to insolvency] after recognition of a foreign main proceeding

Article 29. Coordination of a proceeding under [identify laws of the enacting State relating to insolvency] and a foreign proceeding

Article 30. Coordination of more than one foreign proceeding

Article 31. Presumption of insolvency based on recognition of a foreign main proceeding

Article 32. Rule of payment in concurrent proceedings

---

[251] JOLANTA KREN KOSTIKIEWICZ/RODRIGO RODRIGUEZ, op. cit., p. 192.

X. Cross-border company structures

1. Introduction

Groups of companies have been traditionally widespread in Europe and in the USA. Companies look for diversification. Different companies, under a sole main ownership, may be created in order to operate in different business areas (e.g., food, pharma, construction). The financial results of each business may be effectively monitored if each entity, in the form of a separate company, has its own accounting system and presents its own financial statements. The group structure may also help to attract partners. Minority shareholders (and creditors) can be easily involved if they are allowed to choose whether to provide capital (or financing) to a single business (i.e., only the food sector, pharma sector). Tax laws and the effects of taxation are also a frequent driver for the creation of a group of companies.[252]

Thus, when it comes to cross-border company structures, not only legal but also business management issues are involved. Furthermore, when crossing the border, the company leaves its own national law and enters the scope of application of foreign national and international legal systems. The challenges are manifold and complex. Whether and to what extent a cross-border business activity requires structural adjustments in the company and how these can be designed will be examined in more detail below. The first step is to clarify at what point and in what form a company does business internationally, i.e., across national borders. In a second step, it must be examined whether and how the company's management can anchor this internationality in the company organizationally. In this respect, competencies, knowledge transfers, responsibilities, etc. must be clarified. Organizationally, such an international commitment can therefore be reflected in the corporate structure both in the operational area and in the legal form of the company.[253]

---

[252] ANDREA VICARI, European Company Law (2021), pp. 165-166.
[253] HEIKE DRENCKHAN, Grenzüberschreitende Unternehmensstrukturen, in: Handbuch Internationales Handels- und Wirtschaftsrecht, Rechtliche Herausforderungen im Auslandsgeschäft (2015), p. 442-443.

2. Internationalization

2.1. Generally

A cross-border corporate structure presupposes international activities on the part of the company, i.e., business activities across national borders.

2.2. Company

An unambiguous definition of the term *"company"* is difficult as the term is often used colloquially to refer to corporations, cooperatives, sole proprietors, partnerships etc. Therefore, for the following explanations, the term *"company"* shall be understood as a legal entity that encompasses persons and material resources in pursuit of a purpose.[254] This description alone makes it clear that a company can appear on the market in many different ways.[255]

2.3. Internationalized Company

If a company becomes internationally active, it develops a business activity across national borders. Internationalization is an ambiguous term and is traditionally equated with export. A study by the European Commission showed that export and import are the most common forms of internationalization. These classic first steps across the border are still of immense importance. However, it is to be expected that cross-border cooperations, alliances and networks will become increasingly important.[256]

As a rule, a company brings together five main activities. These are in-house logistics, production, procurement and distribution logistics, marketing & sales and after-sales service. In addition, there are supporting activities such as

---

[254] JEAN NICHOLAS DRUEY/EVA DRUEY JUST/LUKAS GLANZMANN, Handels- und Gesellschaftsrecht (2010), § 1 N 55.
[255] DRENCKHAN, op. cit., p. 443.
[256] EUROPEAN COMMISSION, SMES OBSERVATORY REPORT 2003/4, Internationalization of a SMEs, p. 7.

corporate infrastructure, human resources management, and technology development. Internationalization can affect any of these areas. For example, the knowledge acquired by doing export can be of enormous importance abroad for marketing and product development, thus strengthening the company's competitiveness. Therefore, internationalization should not only be understood as the intention to sell products on foreign markets. Rather, it should be based on an approach that takes into account the entire supply chain and the various forms of internationalization. Accordingly, internationalization is a transnational expansion of entrepreneurial activity. Internationalization is any type of entrepreneurial activity in one or more foreign markets. The company crosses national borders and becomes active on foreign markets. Internationalization understood in this way is not a rigid state, but a dynamic process that begins with one step, entails further steps and changes continuously.[257]

3. Forms of internationalization

There is not one right way to go abroad, but a multitude of possibilities. From the available possibilities, the entrepreneur must choose the form that best suits his company, his product, the chosen strategy and the target country. The following illustration shows possible paths for the entrepreneur. However, on the one hand, this illustration is not exhaustive and on the other hand, the various forms of internationalization can also be combined with each other. For example, it would be conceivable for a company to set up a subsidiary abroad and at the same time sell another product in the same country with the help of a cooperation partner.[258]

---

[257] DRENCKHAN, op. cit., pp. 443-444.
[258] Cf. DRENCKHAN, op. cit., p. 444.

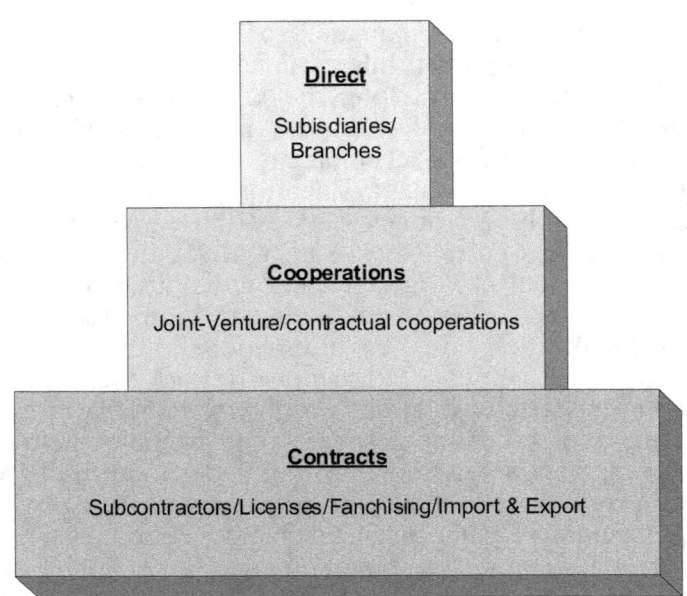

It is essential that the entrepreneur defines a strategy for internationalization and chooses the form of market entry that suits his plan. The product and the target country will not insignificantly influence his decision. The form of internationalization should correspond on the one hand to the chosen strategy and on the other hand to his resources. It is important to find out where the resources will be used, what kind of resources there will be and how high the personnel and financial costs will be. The following chart gives an overview of the different variants of internationalization, the resources to be used in each case and their type. In the case of exports, the effort required is low both financially and in terms of personnel and increases with the complexity of the form of internationalization. Depending on the form of internationalization, the associated risks and the parent company's ability to control foreign operations vary. For example, a subsidiary abroad requires the greatest commitment, but it has its own reputation and the parent's ability to control the foreign business is high. These factors must be taken into account and weighed against each other when making a decision. It should be kept in mind that, despite all the considerations, the risk of a wrong decision cannot be completely ruled out. Therefore, one should consider the possibility that the once chosen form has to be abandoned again and a new path has to be taken. Such changes of direction must remain possible, even if a certain amount of personnel and financial effort cannot be avoided.[259]

Variations of internationalization[260]

	Commitment of resources		Risk		Control possibility
	employees	financial	financial	reputation	
Export	L	L	L	L	H
Licensing Franchising	L	-	-	H	L
Cooperation Joint Ventures	M to H	M	M	M	M to H
Foreign Branch Business establishment	M	M to H	M	M	H
Foreign subsidiary	H	H	H	H	H

L = low; M = medium; H = high

4. Stage theory

Studies show that internationalization occurs in stages. Internationalization usually starts with a low level of commitment and develops into a high level of commitment. As a rule, the starting signal is given with the commencement of export activities to a neighboring country. If these transactions are successful, the company builds up a sales organization abroad, gains experience and later possibly establishes its own subsidiary abroad. In the process, the use of resources increases with each stage. The gradual development has its advantages, because it allows the entrepreneur to gain initial experience abroad. The use of resources and the risks are manageable. In this way, a company can approach cross-border activities in a rather

---

[259] DRENCKHAN, op. cit., pp. 444-445.
[260] Cf. MAGAZINE "*BILANZ*", Zurich 2010, p. 8.

safe environment. The following depiction shows the use of resources at home and abroad depending on the form of internationalization. Whereas in the case of exporting, resources are used primarily in the domestic market, the subsidiary abroad requires human and financial resources.[261]

Stage model of internationalization

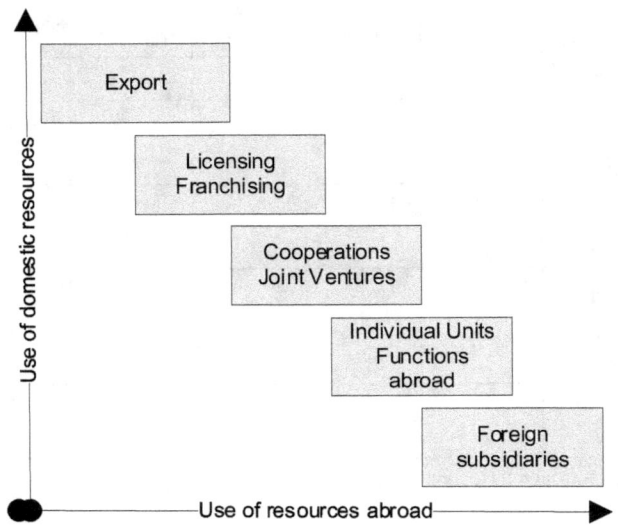

Use of resources at home and abroad depending on the form of internationalization[262]

Even though the step-by-step proceeding described above is a tried and tested approach for most companies, there are still those that remain at one stage or even skip stages.[263] This includes the so-called *"born global"* companies, which dare to take the first steps abroad right from their creation, become active in several countries at the same time or start right away with a more resource-intensive form of

---

[261] MICHAEL KUTSCHKER/STEFAN SCHMID, Internationales Management (2011), pp. 466 et seq.; RALPH LEHMANN, Internationale Markterschliessung, in: Paul Ammann/Ralph Lehmann/Samuel Van den Berg/Christian Hauser, Going International (2012), pp. 71 et seq.

[262] HANS GÜNTHER MEISSNER/STEPHAN GERBER, Die Auslandsinvestitionen als Entscheidungsproblem, Betriebswirtschaftliche Forschung und Praxis, 3/1989, pp. 217-228.

[263] KUTSCHKER/SCHMID, op. cit., p. 249.

internationalization. Despite the very different approaches, it should be noted that the most common form of internationalization, especially among small and medium-sized enterprises (SMEs), is still exporting, and branches or joint ventures abroad are much less common in this segment.[264]

5. Operational organizational structures

5.1. Generally

The explanations above have shown that the first steps across a country's borders regularly require few resources and will therefore hardly be reflected in the company's organizational structure. The company buys products abroad or imports services from abroad. Only when a significant part of the value creation takes place abroad then this commitment will also be reflected organizationally in the company as a whole. A distinction must be made between the statutory and the operational organizational structure:

- The *statutory structure* is concerned with the legal relationships between the foreign branch or subsidiary and the parent company. It is concerned with group growth through business startups, shareholdings or acquisitions (mergers and acquisitions).
- In contrast, the *operational organizational structure* focuses on the business distribution of tasks, competencies and the corresponding responsibilities. These operational processes may well deviate from the statutory structure.

If the foreign commitment assumes a dimension which the company must also take into account in organizational terms, a large number of alternatives can be found in practice as to how companies attempt to meet these requirements. Some of the possibilities are presented in the following overview, although it should be noted that they are rarely encountered in practice in this pure form.[265]

---

[264] EUROPEAN COMMISSION, SMES OBSERVATORY REPORT 2003/4, Internationalization of a SMEs, p. 14 and DRENCKHAN, op. cit., p. 447.

5.2. Non-specific organizational structure

Particularly in the initial phase of foreign operations or when they are of only minor importance, they are hardly reflected in the organizational structure of the company. However, as soon as greater value is created abroad, organizational reorganization must be considered. Even if a first foreign branch or even a subsidiary exists, the managing director or branch manager will regularly still have considerable decision-making scope and report directly to the company management (*"direct reporting"*). Often, this direct-reporting structure is maintained even if further subsidiaries follow.[266]

The *advantages* of such a structure are obvious:
– low expenses;
– flexibility;
– rapid response to local needs;
– good information for management;
– knowledge transfer.

But the *disadvantages* must also be taken into account:
– increased burden on company management;
– strong autonomy of the subsidiary;
– little exchange between subsidiaries;
– personal preferences of the company management regularly have an impact.[267]

In order to counteract in practice the disadvantages just described, it is not uncommon for a foreign business to be linked to the sales or procurement area or to be managed via the administration or finance area or by a separate staff unit. If foreign activities continue to grow, the importance of the export department increases and a process of reorganization can be triggered.[268]

---

[265] DRENCKHAN, op. cit., p. 447.
[266] KUTSCHKER/SCHMID, op. cit., pp. 496-497.
[267] Cf. also KUTSCHKER/SCHMID, op. cit., pp. 496 et seq.
[268] DRENCKHAN, op. cit., p. 448.

5.3. Differentiated organizational structure

It is not uncommon for foreign business to grow initially in an international division which is organizationally separated from the domestic business. For example, in a functional structure a separate department for international activities is created apart from the functional divisions like procurement, selling, production and finances on the same level. [269]

Separate organization of international and domestic business[270]

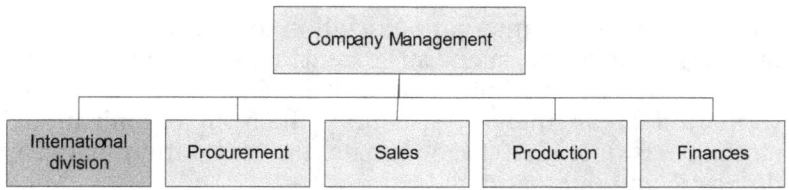

The *advantages* of such a structure are:
- specialization;
- bundling of knowledge and experience;
- short communication and decision-making channels.

The *disadvantages* are:
- isolation tendencies;
- little transfer of know-how to company management;
- duplication of staff departments.[271]

In such cases, it is not uncommon to find a foreign holding company. All foreign activities are combined in a separate legally independent company and managed as a profit center. The economic success of the foreign business is determined, reported and evaluated separately.[272]

---

[269] Cf. DRENCKHAN, op. cit., p. 448.
[270] DRENCKHAN, op. cit., p. 448.
[271] DIRK HOLTBRÜGGE, Internationale Unternehmen, Organisation, in: Georg Schreyögg/Axel von Werder, Enzyklopädie der Betriebswirtschaftslehre/HWO – Handwörterbuch Unternehmensführung und Organisation (2004), p. 2.
[272] HARTMUT KREIKEBAUM/DIRK GILBERT/GLENN O. REINHARDT, Organisationsmanagement internationaler Unternehmen, Grundlagen und Strukturen (2002), pp. 124 et seq.

This type of organizational structure is therefore only recommended if the foreign activities have not yet assumed a significant scale, the degree of diversification of the foreign business is low and only a few managers with international experience are available.[273]

5.4 Integrated organizational structure

5.4.1. Generally

As the degree of internationalization increases, a foreign business grows to such an extent that an international division will be overburdened with it. This gives rise to the formation of an integral structure. Such an organizational structure is intended to eliminate the separation between domestic and international business.[274]

5.4.2. Integrated functional structure

In the integrated functional structure, foreign operations are part of functional divisions. [275]

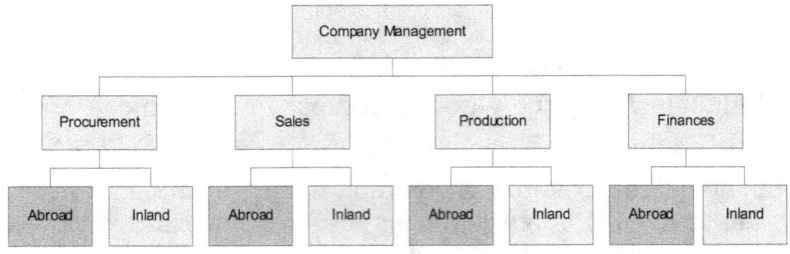

Such a structure appears *advantageous* with regard to the following aspects:
– worldwide coordination in the main functions;
– low management costs.

Such an organization could be *disadvantageous* if

---

[273] Cf. HOLTBRÜGGE, op. cit., p. 2.
[274] DRENCKHAN, op. cit., p. 449.
[275] Cf. DRENCKHAN, op. cit., p. 449.

- the foreign subsidiary or branch is not clearly assigned to a functional area;
- increased coordination requirements and thus an increased burden on the parent company becomes necessary.[276]

Such corporate structures are mostly found in companies whose product differentiation is low and whose foreign activities are still relatively insignificant or limited to exports.[277]

5.4.3. Integrated product structure

In the integrated product structure, foreign activities are assigned to the respective product division. Domestic and foreign companies manufacturing the same products are assigned to the home product division and managed as profit centers.[278]

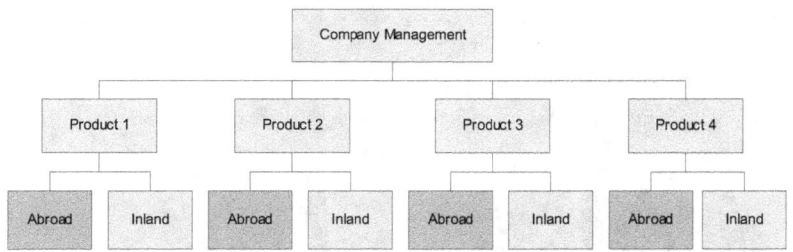

This organizational structure offers *advantages* such as:
- worldwide product coordination;
- consolidation of worldwide market and product know-how;
- organization as a profit center.

Disadvantages could include:
- insufficient consideration of regional specifics;
- more difficult coordination of multi-division subsidiaries;

---

[276] KUTSCHKER/SCHMID, op. cit., p. 507.
[277] Cf. HOLTBRÜGGE, op. cit., p. 2.
[278] HOLTBRÜGGE, op. cit, p. 3 and DRENCKHAN, op. cit., p. 450.

- duplication of resources in the various product categories.[279]

Such corporate organizations are frequently found in companies that have a highly diversified product range at home and abroad.[280]

5.4.4. Integrated regional structure

Another integrated organizational structure is that by *geographic region*. The top level is subdivided by regions, each of whose management is responsible for a specific geographic area. Such an organization is suitable for companies that have a broad geographic base and whose foreign sales account for a high proportion of total profits.[281]

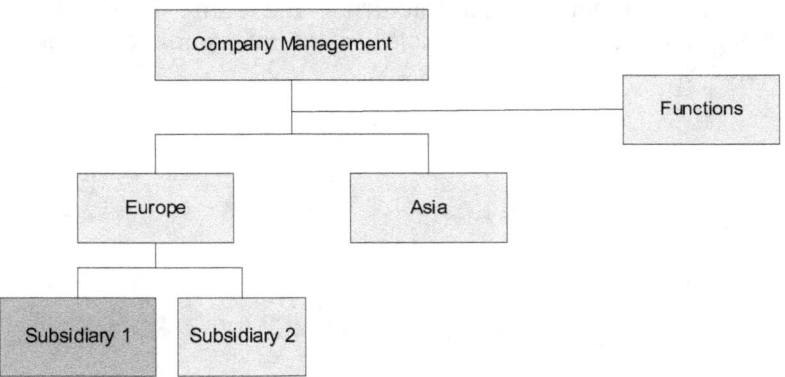

This organizational structure offers *advantages* such as:

- development of know-how for a specific market;
- consideration of regional differences;
- enables response to environmental and market requirements for a specific area.

Disadvantages could include:

- more difficult transfer of product ideas and market experience from one region to another;
- additional costs for regional management level;

---

[279] KUTSCHKER/SCHMID, op. cit., pp. 511 et seq.
[280] HOLTBRÜGGE, op. cit, p. 3.
[281] Cf. DRENCKHAN, op. cit., p. 451.

- regional autonomy is strengthened, making global marketing more difficult.[282]

5.4.5. Multidimensional structures

One-dimensional structures have the weakness of focusing on one structural feature at a time, either functions, product groups, or the respective regions. For this reason, combined structures have often been introduced in practice to counteract this weakness.[283]

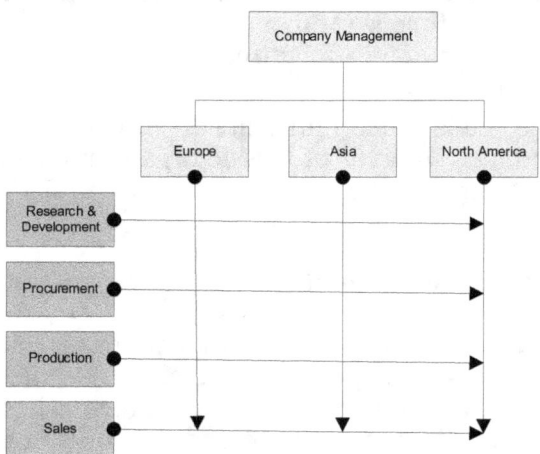

The depiction shows a two-dimensional *matrix structure*. The breakdown by region is combined with the allocation by function.[284] However, a combination of regions and product groups is also possible. For example, at the level below management, both a product manager and an area manager can be found, who develop the product-market strategy with joint responsibility. A further development of the above two-dimensional structure is the three-dimensional grid structure. In this respect, there is regularly a combination of all three levels: function, space and product. Such an organization aims at taking into account the different product

---

[282] DRENCKHAN, op. cit., p. 451.
[283] Cf. DRENCKHAN, op. cit., p. 451.
[284] MANFRED PERLITZ, Internationales Management (2004), p. 622.

requirements in the various countries while at the same time providing central product coordination.[285]

Multidimensional structures seem *advantageous*:
- coordination process promotes communication and creativity;
- expertise takes precedence over hierarchical position
- all dimensions are responsible for profitability;
- increase in the profitability of the products.

Disadvantages could include:
- delimitation of competences and decision-making;
- complexity of the system;
- intensive communication effort;
- high coordination effort.[286]

In practice, such three-dimensional structures have often been abandoned in favor of classic organizational structures because of their complexity.

5.4.6. International holding

More recently, newer organizational forms have been developing the attempt to reflect the requirements of globally operating multinational companies. These include management holding companies and networks. The holding company acquires stakes in more or less independent foreign companies. Such holding companies are the financial holding company, the strategic management holding company and the operational management holding company. A holding structure is found in highly diversified groups in which the parent company concentrates on a few administrative activities.[287]

---

[285] DRENCKHAN, op. cit., p. 452.
[286] KUTSCHKER/SCHMID, op. cit., p. 452.
[287] Cf. DRENCKHAN, op. cit., p. 453.

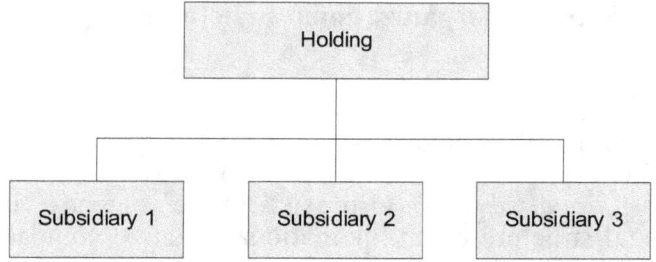

Advantages are certainly:
- low overhead costs of central administration;
- control of loss compensation possible within the group;
- possibly favorable financing possibilities within the group;
- risk distribution among the subsidiaries.

Disadvantages include:
- subsidiary bears the risk of a sale by the parent company;
- little knowledge transfer between parent and subsidiary;
- little synergy between group companies;
- loss of control.[288]

5.4.7. Network structure

Network structures are one of the more recent developments. It is not uncommon for large companies to break up their existing structure and the resulting subunits to work together as networks. SMEs are also increasingly joining together in networks to strengthen their competitiveness. Networks exist in many different forms: circular, star-shaped or in the form of a pyramid.[289]

Such networks can exist as one company. Then it is an intraorganizational network. However, it is also possible for a network to extend beyond the boundaries of the company. In this respect, it is also referred to as an inter-organizational network.[290]

---

[288] Cf. DRENCKHAN, op. cit., p. 453.
[289] KUTSCHKER/SCHMID, op. cit., pp. 534 et seq.
[290] DRENCKHAN, op. cit., p. 453 and KUTSCHKER/SCHMID, op. cit., pp. 535 et seq.

5.5. Statutory organizational structures

5.5.1. Generally

In addition to the operational structure just described, which can be designed in a variety of ways, a *statutory organizational structure* also exists in the company. This is the legal structure of an internationally active company. In some cases, the term legal or shareholding structure is also used. It refers to the legal structure of the company across national borders.[291]

It is not uncommon for the operational structure to differ from the legal structure. While it is possible that organizational and legal entities are congruent, it is also conceivable that legally independent entities comprise several organizational functions. It is possible that certain organizational areas consist of several legal entities. The consequence of such a structure would be that the legal management levels do not necessarily coincide with the operational management functions. The aim of the legal structure is usually the optimal management of financial flows, the minimization of the tax burden and the structuring of liability. However, co-determination rules, the prestige of the legal form and capital procurement possibilities also play a role.[292]

According to the above-mentioned theory of stages, internationalization will usually only be reflected in the articles of association at an advanced stage. If the internationalization reaches a certain extent, so that it should be reflected in the articles of association, the company has two basic options to achieve a stronger structure of the foreign activities. One is to establish a foreign branch office and the other a foreign subsidiary. The latter can take the form of a partnership (e.g., LP) or a corporation (e.g., LLC or a joint stock corporation).[293]

---

[291] DRENCKHAN, op. cit., p. 454 und KUTSCHKER/SCHMID, op. cit., p. 644.
[292] KUTSCHKER/SCHMID, op. cit., p. 649.
[293] Cf. DRENCKHAN, op. cit., p. 454.

5.5.2. Foreign branch office

The company can retain its legal entity and open branches abroad, e.g., as sales or production offices. Such branches are legally dependent of the main establishment, but yet have a certain organizational and economic independence.[294]

For example, in Switzerland, the term branch office is used in the laws but not defined (cf. articles 931 and 952 of the Swiss Code of Obligations). According to the the case law of the Swiss Federal Supreme Court, it is a commercial entity which, although legally part of a main establishment (e.g., company) from which it is dependent, permanently carries on a similar activity in its own premises and thereby has a certain commercial independence.[295]

The point at which a foreign presence becomes a branch office depends on the respective national law. If, for example, the company expands into the EU/EEA area, the Branch Directive (Eleventh Directive 89/666/EEC) regulates the disclosure requirements in a uniform manner. Otherwise, the respective national law applies. Under tax law, such a foreign branch may constitute a permanent establishment.[296]

5.5.2. Foreign subsidiary

Certain functions can be performed by legally independent companies that have a presence in another country (e.g., subsidiary that is producing or distributing goods). Such companies are either founded abroad or acquired through participations in existing companies. The accumulation of independent companies under a single economic management is considered a group.[297]

---

[294] Cf. RINO SIFFERT, Berner Kommentar Handelsregister (2021), Art. 931 N 40 et seq.
[295] Decision of the Swiss Federal Supreme Court 117 II 85 Cons. 3; 108 II 122 Cons. 1 und 89 I 407 Cons. 5.
[296] Cf. DRENCKHAN, op. cit., p. 455.
[297] ROLAND VON BÜREN, Der Konzern, Rechtliche Aspekte eines wirtschaftlichen Phänomens, Schweizerisches Privatrecht, VIII/6 (2005), p. 15.

The formation of a subsidiary is governed by the respective national law of the country in which the subsidiary has its registered office. Usually, a choice can be made between partnerships and corporations. In the case of partnerships, there might be the issue of personal liability on the part of the partners depending the respective national legal system. A corporation, on the other hand, has its own legal personality and its liability is limited to the company's assets. When it comes to setting up a subsidiary in the EU, the parent company can no longer choose the legal dress from national law alone, but according to the case law of the ECJ, the legal forms of all EU member states are also available.[298] In addition, supranational legal forms are available in the EU. These are the European Company (SE, societas europea), the European Economic Interest Grouping (EEIG) and the European Cooperative Society (SCE, societas cooperativa europae).[299]

6. Groups of companies

6.1. Generally

Companies can be linked into a group either by having the same shareholders or directors or by contractual arrangements, in which legally each company is still a separate entity. Of course, it is also possible to link companies in various countries where the management arranges the business in a global context.[300] Although such corporate groups are of immense importance in practice, there are not in every legal system special laws which govern them. Often, the national corporate law has focused solely on the individual independent company. Only in isolated cases are regulations found that are linked to corporate groups, such as the obligation to prepare consolidated financial statements (e.g., article 963 of the Swiss Federal Code of Obligations). Therefore, rules for corporate groups might be derived from doctrine and practice. A group is an *"assembly"* of legally independent

---

[298] DRENCKHAN, op. cit., p. 455.
[299] HECKSCHEN, op. cit., pp. 36 et seq.
[300] JANET DINE/MARIOS KOUTSIAS, Company Law (2020), p. 288.

but economically dependent companies. The group itself does not have active or passive legal capacity. A group can be formed by at least two companies, the parent and the subsidiary. In some cases, the term *"parent company"* and *"subsidiary company"* or *"controlling company"* and *"dependent company"* are also used.[301]

6.2. Management principle

A group exists if several companies are legally independent but economically combined under a single management to form an overall company (so-called *"management principle"*).[302] A group is characterized by uniform management. Such a management can be based on a majority of votes or on contractual, statutory or personal agreements. However, some countries know in their legislation also the so-called *"control principle"* according to which the possibility of controlling another company is sufficient, since it is rarely possible to prove whether influence is actually exercised by the parent company on the subsidiary.[303]

6.3. Group structures

6.3.1. Generally

As we have seen, group structures can offer a variety of advantages like cost savings, optimization of production, logistics and research, or even better utilization of plant/production capacity. Not infrequently, tax incentives such as the holding company privilege or the participation deduction can also be the deciding factor. Corporate groups can arise both *endogenously* and *exogenously*. In the first

---

[301] Cf. VON BÜREN, op. cit., pp. 1 et seq.; DRENCKHAN, op. cit., p. 456 as well as decisions of the Swiss Supreme Court 120 II 331 (*"Swissair-Case"*) and 124 III 297 (*"Motor-Columbus-Case"*).
[302] VON BÜREN, op. cit., p. 5.
[303] Cf. RETO EBERLE, Handkommentar Kommentar Schweizerisches Privatrecht (2016), article 663*e* N 16 and DRENCKHAN, op. cit., p. 456.

case, a parent company establishes a subsidiary. In the second case, existing independent companies are subordinated to another company and integrated, e.g., through the acquisition of shareholdings, joint ventures or a group agreement. Consequently, the structures of international groups are also very individual and shaped by their respective needs.[304]

6.3.2. Parent company structure

The *parent company* is the *"original"* company that stands at the top of the corporate group; it acquires or establishes subsidiaries abroad. The group management and the holding company are combined in the parent company.

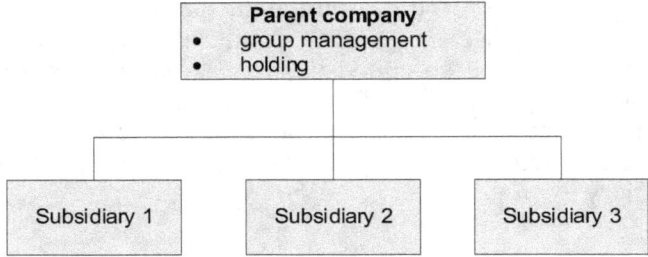

6.3.3. Holding structure

In a holding structure, the *"original"* parent company transfers its shareholdings in the subsidiaries to a holding company which takes over the function of the parent company. Group management can then either remain with the parent company or also be located with the holding. Compared to the parent company solution, the holding company structure offers tax advantages.

---

[304] DRENCKHAN, op. cit., p. 457.

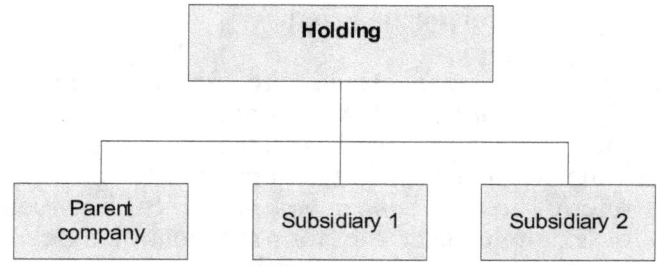

6.3.4. Management company

In the case of the management company, the group management is moved to a separate company, the management company. This company's sole purpose is the group management.

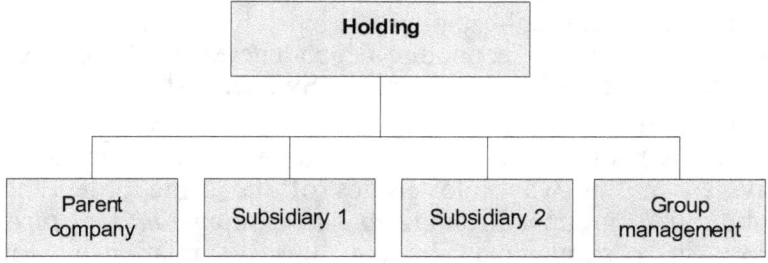

6.3.5. Divisional groups

A divisional group is a group structure with additional subgroups. The group is divided into the various divisions and these individual divisions have their own group management.

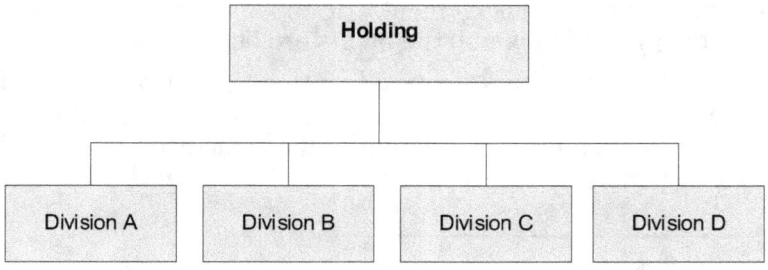

6.4. Types of corporate groups

In addition, corporate groups are further differentiated according to the *nature of their cooperation*. If the legally independent companies work together on the basis of a contract that regulates their relationship with one another, this is referred to as a *contractual group*. Such agreements may, for example, take the form of control agreements, profit pooling agreements, profit transfer agreements, operating lease agreements, operating transfer agreements and voting trust agreements. In contrast, a *de facto group* exists if such agreements do not exist and the cooperation is based solely on the exercise of actual power. Such potential power arises in particular when one company holds the shares in another company. The controlling company can exert its influence through the shares it holds in the subsidiary (so-called *"investment group"*). Further means of control arise through statutory provisions, interlocking of personnel or purely economic dependencies. Such de facto groups are regularly encountered in Switzerland.[305]

Furthermore, a distinction is also made according to the *hierarchy* between the various companies and the groups are divided in this way into groups of the same order and subordinate groups. In a *group with a common structure*, there is a single management, but no relationship of dependency. Several companies stand next to each other on an equal footing. There is a cooperative relationship between them in that the individual companies are subject to a jointly determined top management. Such uniform management can also take the form of a joint advisory board in the form of a simple partnership. More far-reaching and deeper interdependencies exist in the *subordinate group*. There is a relationship of dependency between the companies that goes beyond uniform management. In most cases, there is a parent company on which the others are dependent.[306]

A further distinguishing feature between the various types of corporate group is the *economic level* at which the individual companies operate. If companies at the same economic level work together, this is referred to as a *horizontal group*. A

---

[305] VON BÜREN, op. cit., p. 28.
[306] Cf. VON BÜREN, op. cit., p. 28.

vertical group involves companies under a single management that come from different economic levels. If, in addition, companies from different economic sectors are involved, it is a *diagonal or conglomerate group.* [307]

6.5. Group of companies considered as one legal entity vs. piercing the corporate veil

6.5.1. Generally

As many jurisdictions do not have a specific law regarding groups of companies, the courts as well as the legal doctrine had to discuss whether or not a group of companies is to be regarded as one entity and came to different solutions in the various jurisdictions.

6.5.2. Anglo-Saxon Law

For example, in the UK there is no formal or informal recognition of group interests except in particular situations. In accounting, there are provisions that require that accounts have to be consolidated so that the parent company and the subsidiaries can be taxed together and thus are treated as one unit. However, besides that the UK courts are reluctant to admit the reality of linked companies acting in any way other than as a number of separate entities tied together by their relationship as significant shareholders in each other.[308] Therefore, they generally still apply the principle of separate legal personality specifically to the situation of groups of companies.[309]

---

[307] DRENCKHAN, op. cit., p. 459.
[308] DINE/KOUTSIAS, op. cit., p. 288.
[309] This rule is emanating from the renowned case of SALOMON V SALOMON CO LTD [1896] UKHL, in which the House of Lords unanimously set out the doctrine of corporate personality – if a company is set up in accordance with law it has a separate legal personality distinct from its members.

Adams v. Cape Industries plc ([1990] Ch 433)

"The fundamental principle is that each company in a group of companies is a separate legal entity possessed of separate legal rights and liabilities."

Southard & Company Ltd Re ([1979] EWCA Civ J0627-3)

Lord Judge Templeman noted in the aforementioned case concerning groups of companies that parent companies, other subsidiaries and shareholders of an indebted company, are not to be held responsible for the liabilities of an indebted company within a group.

However, this point of view can be harmful to creditors or third parties. If there is a reasonable belief that the separate legal personality is being used as a means of continuing fraud or the subsidiary is really an extension of the parent company or the shareholders, then the veil between the company and its shareholders can be lifted. This is called *"Piercing the corporate veil"* or also *"Lifting the veil of incorporation"*. It refers to a situation in which courts put aside the principle of separate legal personality and the resulting limited liability and hold the company's shareholders or directors personally liable for the company's actions or debts. It is only where there is a reasonable belief that the separate legal personality is being used as a means of continuing fraud, abusing the company (e.g., intermingling of personal and corporate assets), undercapitalization at the time of incorporation or the subsidiary is really an extension of the owner, that the veil between the company and its shareholders may be lifted.[310]

Smith, Stone and Knight Limited v. Birmingham Corporation ([1939] 4 All ER 116)

In the case of Smith, Stone & Knight Limited v. Birmingham Corporation wherein the Birmingham

---

[310] Cf. Cornell Legal Information Institute, Piercing the Corporate Veil, https://www.law.cornell.edu/wex/piercing_the_corporate_veil.

Corporation expropriated land that had been used by a subsidiary of the claimant, the Court held that the questions that need be asked were:

1. Were the profits treated as profits of the parent?
2. Were the persons conducting the business appointed by the parent?
3. Was the parent the head and brain of the trading venture?
4. Did the parent govern the venture, decide what should be done and what capital should be embarked on the venture?
5. Did the parent make the profits by its skill and direction?
6. Was the parent in effectual and constant control?'

Where prima facie evidence can be shown to answer the above questions in the affirmative, then the courts may lift the corporate veil.

In the US while the law varies from state to state, generally courts have a strong presumption against piercing the corporate veil, and will only do so if there has been serious misconduct. Courts understand the benefits of limited liability, as it *"encourages development of public markets for stocks and thus helps to make possible the liquidity and diversification benefits that investors receive from those markets."* As such, courts typically require corporations to engage in fairly egregious actions in order to justify piercing the corporate veil. In general, creditors have no recourse against corporate shareholders, as long as formalities are satisfied. When, however, the corporation is fraudulently created to escape liability, then creditors may pierce the corporate veil.[311]

Broward Marine, Inc. v. S/V Zeus
(S.D. Fla. Feb. 1, 2010)

In Florida, one must typically show two things in order to pierce the corporate veil:

---

[311] ROBERT B. THOMPSON, Piercing the Corporate Veil: An Empirical Study, 76 Cornell L. Rev. 1036 (1991), p. 1040.

1. That the relevant corporation is only the alter ego or mere instrumental of the parent corporation or its shareholder(s);
2. That the alleged parent company or shareholder(s) also engaged in improper conduct.

Walkovsky v. Carlton
(24 A.D.2d 582 [1965])

The court in that case held that a plaintiff needs to prove that a shareholder used the corporation as his agent to conduct business in an individual capacity. A court will pierce the corporate veil when it finds that the corporation is an agent of its shareholder, and will hold the principal vicariously liable.

In Re Jns Aviation, LLC
(376 B.R. 500 [Bankr. N.D. Tex. 2007])

The court found that the corporate veil could be pierced when any of the asserted veil-piercing strands are met. Further, courts will pierce the corporate veil when the member(s) intended to use the company to perpetrate an actual fraud, and the company did perpetrate an actual fraud *"primarily for the direct personal benefit of the considered defendant."*

To fulfill this requirement, the corporation must be one of three things:

1. The alter ego of the parent corporation or its shareholder(s)
2. The corporation is used to avoid legal limitations upon natural persons or corporations
3. The corporation is a sham to perpetrate a fraud.

Further, the court stated that *"actual fraud"* occurs when all four of the following conditions take place:

1. *"a party conceals or fails to disclose a material fact within the knowledge of that party"*;
2. *"the party knows that the other party is ignorant of the fact and does not have an equal opportunity to discover the truth"*;

3. *"the party intends the other party to take some action by concealing or failing to disclose the fact"*;

4 *"the other party suffers injury as a result of acting without knowledge of the undisclosed fact"*.

6.5.3. European Law

European company law is partially codified in Directive (EU) 2017/1132, and EU member states continue to operate separate company acts, which are amended from time to time to comply with EU directives and regulations. Ongoing efforts towards establishing a modern and efficient company law and corporate governance framework for European undertakings, investors and employees aim to improve the business environment in the EU. However, there is no specific EU law on group of companies. The draft of the ninth company law directive (*"Proposal for a Ninth Directive Based on Article 54(3)(g) of the EEC Treaty on Links Between Undertakings and, in particular, on Groups"*) was aiming at a unification of certain rules concerning groups of companies, but the original proposal, which was strongly oriented towards the German group law, has since been abandoned.[312]

However, despite the fact that there has only been limited harmonization of the rules on groups of companies in the EU, the ECJ has often had to rule on cases in the field of unfair competition involving groups of companies. The ECJ made rulings in which it had to consider on how to treat groups of companies under Union law, including whether to treat a group as a single company or as several companies.[313] According to a consistent practice, it is not only the legal entity that directly violated competition law that can be held

---

[312] HECKSCHEN, op. cit., p. 54. Cf. also KLAUS BÖHLHOFF/JULIUS BUDDE, Company Groups – The EEC proposal for a ninth directive in the light of the legal situation in the Federal Republic of Germany, in: Journal of Comparative Business and Capital Market Law 6 (1984), pp. 163 et seq.

[313] KARSTEN ENGSIG SØRENSEN, Groups of Companies in the Case Law of the Court of Justice of the European Union, in: European Business Law Review Volume 27, Issue 3 (2016), pp. 393 et seq.

liable, but also the parent company, provided it has exerted *"decisive influence"*. The liability of other legal entities that are part of the *"economic unit"* are also debated in these court decisions. Company lawyers have sharply criticized this practice, as it amounts to a *"piercing of the corporate veil"* beyond established company law principles.[314]

> **Biogaran v. European Commission (Case T-677/14)**
>
> The concept of companies being treated collectively as a single undertaking is the solution adopted by European competition (or antitrust) law to the problem which arises when different people in a corporate group act in concert to commit a wrong. The court confirmed that the single undertaking analysis works in both directions, both up and down the corporate chain. Accordingly, if a subsidiary is in the same undertaking as its parent, then the parent's wrongdoing is also the subsidiary's wrongdoing. Thus, Biogaran's complaint, that it was wrongly being held liable for an infringement carried out by its parent (the French pharmaceutical giant Servier), was rejected.[315]

EU rules also require certain large companies, which are most of the times head or part of a group of companies, to report annually on the social and environmental impacts and risks related to their activities. This helps investors, civil society organizations, consumers, policymakers and other stakeholders to evaluate the non-financial performance of large companies and encourages companies to develop a responsible approach to business. The new EU Corporate Sustainability Reporting Directive contains rules on the disclosure of financial and diversity information by certain large companies, which are most of the times head or part of a group of companies. These cover – as we have seen - areas

---

[314] HEIKE SCHWEIZTER/KAI WOESTE, Die Haftung von Konzerngesellschaften im europäischen Wettbewerbsrecht, Der wettbewerbsrechtliche Unternehmensbegriff und seine Legitimationsgrundlagen, in: Vom Konzern zum Einheitsunternehmen (2020), pp. 141 et seq.

[315] Cf. also TRISTAN JONES, EU competition law: the liability of group companies for each other's wrongdoing, in: Butterworths Journal of International Banking and Financial Law, March 2019, pp. 184-185.

such as environmental matters, social matters and the treatment of employees, respect for human rights, anti-corruption and bribery, and diversity on company boards (e.g., age, gender, educational and professional background).

6.5.4. Swiss Law

Also in Switzerland, the principle of separate legal personality of a company within a group of companies is still applied. There is no codified law on groups of companies in the Swiss legal system. However, the Swiss Code of Obligations contains individual provisions on matters relating to corporate groups, e.g., in the area of accounting (article 663*e* et seq. CO), regarding the acquisition of treasury shares (article 659*b* CO) or in the Swiss Merger Act regarding the parent-subsidiary-merger or between subsidiaries of the same group under simplified conditions. In addition, the Swiss Federal Supreme Court has developed a differentiated case law which takes into account the reality of corporate groups. Based on general principles of corporate law, the practice of the court has conceived specific solutions for affiliated companies, such as for the question of liability within the group (so-called "*piercing the corporate veil*").

Swissair
(Decision of the Swiss Federal Supreme Court 120 II 331, 336 et seq.)
Under certain circumstances, created trust in the parent company's conduct within the group can be a basis for liability even in the absence of a contractual or tortious basis for liability. This results from a generalization of the principles on liability from *culpa in contrahendo*, i.e., there is a liability of the parent company if the parent company, through its conduct, raises certain expectations, but later disappoints them in breach of good faith. In this case, the parent company is liable for the damage which it has caused in an adequately causal manner by its conduct in breach of good faith.

In principle, it corresponds to a legitimate need of the economy to be able to outsource the risk of the individual business divisions to subsidiaries and thereby limit the liability to their assets. Any abuses might be subject to legal claims based on the piercing the corporate veil-doctrine and even be covered by criminal law norms.

7. Power of multinational companies

7.1. Generally

There are three principal reasons why multinational companies became so powerful:
– the veil of incorporation;
– large-scale production; and
– extraterritoriality.[316]

7.2. The veil of incorporation

In many jurisdictions, companies of a group are considered each as a separate legal entity (e.g., in the UK, USA, EU and Switzerland). In many countries – as we have seen – the courts have been very reluctant to lift the veil between a parent company and a subsidiary. However, limited liability was a notion implemented by law in order to shift the risk between investors (shareholders), creditors and other stakeholders. In the light of corporate governance, the shareholders are the most powerful stakeholders in the company. They usually take only the risk that they might lose their invested money; they are protected from losing their other assets, including their houses. At the same time, they might get dividends from the company. The protection of shareholders gives them a cushion, which can be used to speculate. This is the basic tenet of capitalism. Often, the investment fuels other businesses that will be linked with the initial company; often, this is the reason for the foundation of multinational companies. Once the linked companies are established, they become powerful, sometimes pushing smaller companies into insolvency. When the USSR fell, the capitalist West was emboldened to believe that capitalism

---

[316] DINE/KOUTSIAS, op. cit., p. 294.

was the only possible system. This led to a loss of checks and balances for stakeholders in companies, with the shareholders and the directors becoming very powerful. However, many people believe that multinational companies are not regulated enough, allowing directors' salaries and shareholders' dividends to rise enormously.[317]

7.3. Large-scale production

Having a number of companies linked together allows them to consolidate their business, making them more efficient. For example, if a parent company and several subsidiaries merge their administration and their chain of production, the product that they manufacture will be cheaper because the costs will be less. They will not employ as many people and in chain of production their transport costs will be shared. This means that their competitors will be at a disadvantage, and eventually they will have to either cut their prices or reduce expenses in their business. Otherwise, they will become insolvent.[318]

7.4. Extraterritoriality

As a company group grows, it will often export its products into other jurisdictions. Thus, the parent company will often incorporate a subsidiary in the countries where the business is to be found. This will allow the group to expand and this will mean further efficiency savings. Such savings will be not only in the business itself but also in tax advantages. Within a group, assets can be switched between companies, allowing them to trade between themselves. This is known as 'transfer pricing'. Theoretically, the asset should be evaluated by an 'arm's length' evaluation. However, there is a serious conflict of interests in these negotiations and the tax authorities in each jurisdiction need to regulate such transactions. In a poor country, this is problematic because the local authorities might not have the resources to police the transfers adequately. In all countries in these situations,

---

[317] Cf. DINE/KOUTSIAS, op. cit., p. 295.
[318] DINE/KOUTSIAS, op. cit., pp. 295 et seq.

there is a serious risk of corruption. This may amount to simple bribery, but more subtle conflicts of interests can occur; for example, where a government wishes to promote a company for regional or national advantages, it might change the tax rate for that particular company. The EU tries to prevent these abuses, but multinational companies are acting global now. Frequently, in the case of environmental hazards or labor abuses, including health and safety violations, a parent company can hive off risky or dirty business abroad. Problematically, the subsidiary company will generally not be sued, either because the venture is in a state that is politically unstable and/or lacking in effective environmental regulation or enforcement practices or because the subsidiary can be starved of finance by the parent and placed in danger of insolvency. Meanwhile, suing the parent company is problematic because each company in the multinational company group is construed as completely separate. Each jurisdiction, moreover, has a limited jurisdictional reach, while, in effect, each company in the multinational company group is insulated by the operation of the 'corporate veil', isolating the companies making up the group. In this sense, the multinational company makes a particularly complex target for the imposition of liability: there is no single multinational company 'entity' as such.[319]

---

[319] DINE/KOUTSIAS, op. cit., p. 296.

www.ingramcontent.com/pod-product-compliance
Lightning Source LLC
Chambersburg PA
CBHW052347220526
45465CB00003BA/998